Praise for *Agenda for a New Economy*

"David Korten tells the truth like no one else—a truth our planet needs us to hear."

> Marjorie Kelly, cofounder, Corporation 20/20; founding editor, *Business Ethics* magazine; and author of *The Divine Right of Capital*

"Korten turns conventional economic thinking upside down and inside out. This book reveals what is really going on in the U.S. and global economies—and what can and should be done about it."

> Van Jones, founder and president, Green for All, and author of *The Green Collar Economy*

"David Korten shows that patching the tires of a vehicle that's going over a cliff is neither sane nor acceptable. But the financial crisis can be a healing crisis, and Korten gives us prescriptions that could actually give us a thriving and just economy that works for people and the planet. I hope every reader feels a sense of relief at hearing the truth and a renewed passion for civic engagement, now knowing what direction we need to steer our ship."

> Vicki Robin, coauthor of *Your Money or Your Life* and cofounder, Conversation Cafés

"A great book. Korten provides solutions far beyond economics. If we care about the health, safety, education, and well-being of our society and want to create a world with a semblance of social and economic equity, this book is the next big step in that direction."

> Peter Block, author of *Community* and *Stewardship*

"David Korten gives us the big picture here. More than just firing a provocative salvo at the dangerous misconceptions that got us into the current economic mess, Korten taps into thousands of years of human history for deeper insight into the myths that have persisted in sowing exploitation and division. He is lighting the way toward a new, human-centered conception of what it really means to be rich."

> Lee Drutman, coauthor of *The People's Business*

"Korten has zeroed in on the real problem of Wall Street and how to stop the plunder and pillaging of our economy."

> Edward Winslow, founder, Protect Money Investments, and author of *Blind Faith*

"The most important book to emerge thus far on the economic crisis. David Korten provides real solutions."

> Peter Barnes, cofounder, Working Assets, and author of *Capitalism 3.0*

"Building upon his earlier explorations of economics, history, and psychology, Korten explains why Washington's response to the current economic crisis is like trying to put a fire out with gasoline. By outlining a foundational framework for extricating the economy from the clutches of Wall Street and creating a real-wealth New Economy based on Main Street, Korten provides essential guideposts for those working for real change."

Charlie Cray, Director, *Center for Corporate Policy*

"At last, a book by one of our most brilliant economic thinkers that outlines the real causes of—and solutions to—the current economic crisis! David Korten has devoted his professional life to analyzing the strengths and weaknesses of the global economic system. Now he draws on his extensive knowledge to inspire us, we the people, to take actions that will create a more just and sustainable world for ourselves and future generations.

John Perkins, *New York Times* bestselling author of *Confessions of an Economic Hit Man* and *The Secret History of the American Empire*

"No one should be surprised that David Korten is the first great thinker to assemble a detailed road map for a new economy where people, the planet, and communities come first. He replaces fear and anxiety with clarity and hope."

John Cavanagh, Director, Institute for Policy Studies

"David Korten has provided an economic blueprint for the 21st century. Just as the global economy crumbles, Korten's timely plan for a new economy—a locally based living economy—will keep Spaceship Earth on a steady course, while bringing greater equality and strengthening our democratic institutions. And as if that were not enough, it will bring us more joy."

Judy Wicks, cofounder and chair, Business Alliance for Local Living Economies

"A stirring defense of life and liberty. Guided by the hand of Adam Smith, David Korten paints a spirited picture of a new economy: in bold strokes, from the Earth up, and for all the people. Obama watchers, take note—page after page, redesign trumps reform and shouts, 'Yes, we can!'"

Raffi Cavoukian, singer, author, entrepreneur, ecology advocate, and founder of Child Honoring

To Margaret

AGENDA
FOR A **NEW**
ECONOMY

From PHANTOM WEALTH
to REAL WEALTH

Thanks for your great work.

DAVID C. KORTEN

BK

Berrett–Koehler Publishers, Inc.
San Francisco
a BK Currents book

Berrett-Koehler Publishers, Inc.
235 Montgomery Street, Suite 650
San Francisco, CA 94104-2916
Tel: (415) 288-0260   Fax: (415) 362-2512   www.bkconnection.com

ORDERING INFORMATION

QUANTITY SALES. Special discounts are available on quantity purchases by corporations, associations, and others. For details, contact the "Special Sales Department" at the Berrett-Koehler address above.

INDIVIDUAL SALES. Berrett-Koehler publications are available through most bookstores. They can also be ordered directly from Berrett-Koehler:
Tel: (800) 929-2929; Fax: (802) 864-7626; www.bkconnection.com

ORDERS FOR COLLEGE TEXTBOOK/COURSE ADOPTION USE. Please contact Berrett-Koehler: Tel: (800) 929-2929; Fax: (802) 864-7626.

ORDERS BY U.S. TRADE BOOKSTORES AND WHOLESALERS. Please contact Ingram Publisher Services, Tel: (800) 509-4887; Fax: (800) 838-1149; E-mail: customer.service@ingrampublisherservices.com; or visit www.ingrampublisherservices.com/Ordering for details about electronic ordering.

Berrett-Koehler and the BK logo are registered trademarks of Berrett-Koehler Publishers, Inc.

Printed in the United States of America

Berrett-Koehler books are printed on long-lasting acid-free paper. When it is available, we choose paper that has been manufactured by environmentally responsible processes. These may include using trees grown in sustainable forests, incorporating recycled paper, minimizing chlorine in bleaching, or recycling the energy produced at the paper mill.

CIP data is available from the Library of Congress.

ISBN 978-1-60509-289-8 (pbk.)
ISBN 978-1-60509-290-4 (PDF e-book)

First Edition
14 13 12 11 10 09   10 9 8 7 6 5 4 3 2 1

Project management and book design by Valerie Brewster, copyediting by Karen Seriguchi, proofreading by Todd Manza.

CONTENTS

▶•◆•◆•◀

To Steve Piersanti and the incredible staff of Berrett-Koehler, who proposed this book project and supported it above and beyond

To the staff and board of *YES!* magazine, who are communicating a new vision of human possibility to the world

To the staff, board, and local network members of the Business Alliance for Local Living Economies (BALLE), who are building the New Economy

To the staff of the Institute for Policy Studies, who are helping to frame the New Economy policy agenda and to build a supportive political alliance

To the hundreds of grassroots groups engaged in popular economics education and political mobilization

And to the buccaneers and privateers of Wall Street, including poster boy Bernard Madoff, whose excesses revealed a financial system so corrupt and detached from reality as to be beyond repair; without them, this call to shut down Wall Street would surely have fallen on deaf ears

PREFACE

The Wall Street implosion in 2008 and the failure of the subsequent bailout effort present an unparalleled opportunity to open a long-overdue national conversation around some basic yet previously unasked questions.

1. Do Wall Street institutions do anything so vital for the national interest that it justifies opening the national purse strings to shower them with trillions of dollars to save them from the consequences of their own excess?

2. Is it possible that the whole Wall Street edifice is built on an illusion that has no substance yet carries deadly economic, social, and environmental consequences for the larger society?

3. Might there be other ways to provide necessary and beneficial financial services with greater effectiveness and at lesser cost?

To break the suspense, here are the answers: (1) no, (2) yes, (3) yes.

Most public discussion of the financial crisis has focused on finger-pointing. Who engaged in criminal activity? Who was responsible for falsifying securities ratings? Who was responsible for rolling back essential regulations? Which regulators were asleep at the switch and why? Many have called for stronger rules and closer oversight. A few—notably Dean Baker (*Plunder and Blunder*), Kevin Phillips (*Bad Money*), and Charles Morris (*The Trillion Dollar Meltdown*)—have extensively documented the corruption of Wall Street's most powerful institutions.

I have yet to read or hear any commentator, including Baker, Phillips, or Morris, suggest that the solution to the financial crisis is to let go of Wall Street and build a new economy based on different values and institutions.

I have written *Agenda for a New Economy* to break the silence and open a discussion of this so far unmentioned possibility. It is addressed specifically to people who want to deepen their understanding of why things are going so badly wrong economically, socially, and environmentally and who are looking for real solutions that go beyond putting temporary patches on failed institutions.

Here in brief is the somewhat unusual story of how this book came to be.

In the fall of 2008, Rabbi Michael Lerner invited me to write an article for *Tikkun* magazine reviewing big-think books by two influential economists. With Michael's guidance, the article evolved as the financial meltdown played out, and it ended up as a call for a basic redesign of our economic institutions and a proposed address for delivery by President Obama on a New Economy agenda. As I was working on that piece with Michael, *YES!* magazine editors Sarah van Gelder and Doug Pibel suggested I do a piece for *YES!* that would speak to the bailout passed by Congress but would also go beyond to outline an agenda for a new economy. The *Tikkun* and *YES!* articles both appeared shortly after the November 2008 presidential election. They set the stage for writing this book, and I have freely adapted material from both in its writing. I owe a special debt of gratitude to the editors of these forward-looking magazines for their invitations and guidance, without which this book might never have been written.

Late in the evening on November 24, Steve Piersanti, the president and publisher of Berrett-Koehler Publishers, with whom I've worked on my most widely read books, sent me an e-mail message saying he had read the *YES!* magazine article and wanted to help get its message out far and wide, perhaps as a short book.

My wife, Fran, and I discussed his invitation the next morning and had a phone conversation with Steve that evening, during which we outlined a production schedule to have the book ready to launch on January 23, 2009, immediately following Obama's presidential inauguration. This was the day I was scheduled to deliver a keynote address at a national theological conference sponsored by the historic Trinity Church, located in the heart of Wall Street. We found it difficult to imagine a more propitious time and place to launch a book calling for an end to Wall Street and the altar of mammon.

The idea energized the Berrett-Koehler team, and they and I accepted the challenge. We had eight weeks from starting the project to shipping the books to Trinity in time for the launch. I had to generate the manuscript, drawing from my previous work as appropriate as well as writing a great deal of new material. The editing, design, production, and printing had to be done in a few weeks. Yet through the close collaboration of all parties, the elements came together in an integrated, distinctive, and powerful whole.

Great credit for this goes to the tremendous support I received from the Berrett-Koehler team, Fran, and my other colleagues. Steve Piersanti read every chapter as I drafted it and provided invaluable feedback. Michael Crowley adjusted his holiday vacation time to put together the cover text, endorsements, and marketing materials. Karen Seriguchi, who served as copy editor, worked with me literally around the clock for ten days to produce a final edited text.

The clear deadline, rather like a scheduled execution, helped to focus the mind, as did the book's drive to a clear bottom line: shut down Wall Street and build a new economy on the foundation of Main Street, with a new financial system dedicated to serving its needs.

The tight deadline and clear bottom line also helped me resist the impulse to delve into the complexities of the various

Wall Street financial schemes and scams. Once we are clear that Wall Street is operating an extortion racket that imposes unbearable costs on society while serving no beneficial function not better met in other ways, we really don't need to worry about the arcane details of exactly how the scams work. For those who want the details, there are other books, such as those mentioned above by Baker, Phillips, and Morris. *Agenda for a New Economy* is about the bigger picture.

As I reach the end of this sprint to the publication finishing line, I realize the extent to which I have been preparing my whole life to write this book. I grew up in a conservative small town where I learned to value family, community, and nature and the special character of America as a middle-class democracy, free from the extremes of wealth and poverty that I was led to believe characterized the world's less advanced nations. In my childhood, my dad, a local retail merchant, taught me that if your primary business purpose is not to serve your customers and community, then you have no business being in business. The wilderness experiences of my adolescent years taught me a reverence for nature.

My Stanford Business School education taught me to look for the big picture. My doctoral dissertation research in Ethiopia taught me the power of culture in shaping collective behavior. From my experience as an Air Force captain on the faculty of the Special Air Warfare School and as a military aide in the Office of the Secretary of Defense during the Vietnam War, I learned how the world's most powerful military was thwarted by the self-organizing networks of an ill-equipped peasant army. My tour as a member of the organization faculty at the Harvard Business School helped me understand the dynamics of large-scale organizational systems.

During my years in Asia with the Ford Foundation and the U.S. Agency for International Development, I experienced the positive power and potential of local community self-organization and the importance of local control of essential economic resources. I learned about strategies for large-scale institutional change from my involvement in both successful and unsuccessful efforts to restructure national resource-management systems in irrigation and forestry to place control in the hands of local communities. It was during these fifteen years in Asia that I became aware of a terrible truth: development models based on economic growth were making a few people fabulously wealthy at an enormous social and environmental cost to the substantial majority.

In writing *When Corporations Rule the World*, I came to understand why the publicly traded private-purpose corporation is an inherently destructive anti-market business form. In writing *The Post-Corporate World: Life after Capitalism*, I came to see the important distinction between the Wall Street capitalist economy and Main Street market economies and the ways in which properly designed market systems mimic the organizing dynamics and principles of healthy living systems.

From the experience of my daughters, Diana and Alicia, I saw firsthand how the Wall Street reengineering of the economy has made it much more difficult for today's young professionals to get established economically than it was for my generation.

Through my experience with the International Forum on Globalization and the global resistance against corporate-led economic globalization, I learned how a new story spread by global citizen networks can reshape the course of history. As I pushed deeper in my analysis, I came to see that the power of financial markets trumps even the power of global corporations.

My experience with *YES!* magazine gave new definition to my vision of a possible human future, based on its wealth of stories about people taking practical action to create a world that works for everyone. Writing *The Great Turning: From*

Empire to Earth Community brought historical depth to my understanding of why our species is now in such deep crisis and raised my consciousness of the pervasive presence and perverse consequences of dominator cultures and institutions that nurture and reward behavioral pathology. My experience with the Business Alliance for Local Living Economies inspired my sense of the opportunity at hand to build a just and sustainable New Economy on the foundation of Main Street economies.

All these many themes inform and find expression in *Agenda for a New Economy*. Many of them are developed at greater length in my other books mentioned above.

There are many other resources for those of you interested in the perspective of other current writers who are dealing with important aspects of the New Economy. These are a few of the many that have contributed to my thinking: Michael Shuman, *The Small-Mart Revolution: How Local Businesses Are Beating the Global Competition*; Van Jones, *The Green Collar Economy: How One Solution Can Fix Our Two Biggest Problems*; Riane Eisler, *The Real Wealth of Nations: Creating a Caring Economics*; Bill McKibben, *Deep Economy: The Wealth of Communities and the Durable Future*; and James Gustave Speth, *The Bridge at the Edge of the World: Capitalism, the Environment, and Crossing from Crisis to Sustainability*.

Another valuable resource for those who are looking for more information on the people and organizations engaged in creating the New Economy and other initiatives intended to create just, sustainable, and compassionate societies is *YES!* magazine (yesmagazine.org), which I serve as board chair.

If you want to get involved in developing your local Main Street economy into a model New Economy, two national organizations can be of help: the Business Alliance for Local Living Economies (livingeconomies.org) and the American

Independent Business Alliance (amiba.net). Both are active in the United States and Canada, and both are devoted to strengthening local independent businesses and building their distinctive brand identity.

BALLE has a particular focus on developing relationships among local independent businesses to strengthen what it calls the building blocks of healthy local living economies: sustainable agriculture, green building, renewable energy, community capital, zero-waste manufacturing, and independent retail. I am a member of the BALLE governing board.

AMIBA has paid particular attention to giving local independent businesses a political voice and changing the rules to level the playing field in the competition between local businesses and corporate box stores. I am a member of the AMIBA advisory board.

I cochair with John Cavanagh, executive director of the Institute for Policy Studies (ips-dc.org) in Washington, D.C., a New Economy Working Group formed at the end of 2008 to further develop and advance New Economy policies. IPS, which works in partnership with progressive members of Congress and many national groups involved in economic education and policy advocacy, serves as the secretariat of the Working Group. We expect to have a New Economy Working Group Web site active by the time this book launches (new-economyworkinggroup.org).

You can also find updates on my Web sites—davidkorten.org and greatturning.org. Both provide links to a wealth of additional resources, including a group discussion guide for *Agenda for a New Economy*. You can sign up at either site for our free Great Turning Initiative e-mail newsletter.

David Korten
davidkorten.org

PART I

THE CASE FOR A
NEW ECONOMY

►◄◆►◄◆►◄

If we look upstream for the ultimate cause of the economic crisis that is tearing so many lives apart, we find an illusion: the belief that money—a mere number created with a simple accounting entry that has no reality outside the human mind—is wealth. Because money represents a claim on so many things essential to our survival and well-being, we easily slip into evaluating economic performance in terms of the rate of financial return to money, essentially the rate at which money is growing, rather than by the economy's contribution to the long-term well-being of people and nature.

We can trace each of the major failures of our economic system to the misperception of money as wealth: the boom-and-bust cycles; the decimation of the middle class; families forced to choose between paying the rent, putting food on the table, and caring for their children; the decline of community life; and the wanton destruction of nature.

Once the belief that money is wealth is implanted firmly in the mind, it is easy to accept the idea that money is a storehouse of value rather than simply a storehouse of expectations, and that "making money" is the equivalent of "creating wealth." Because Wall Street makes money in breathtaking quantities, we have allowed it to assume control of the whole economy—and therein lies the source of our problem.

Financial collapse pulled away the curtain on the Wall

Street alchemists to reveal an illusion factory that paid its managers outrageous sums for creating phantom wealth unrelated to the production of anything of real value. They were merely creating claims on the real wealth created by others—a form of theft.

Spending trillions of dollars trying to fix Wall Street is a fool's errand. Our hope lies not with the Wall Street phantom-wealth machine, but rather with the real-world economy of Main Street, where people engage in the production and exchange of real goods and services to meet the real needs of their children, families, and communities, and where they have a natural interest in maintaining the health and vitality of their natural environment.

Ironically, it turns out that the solution to a failed capitalist economy is a real-market economy much in line with the true vision of Adam Smith. Building a new real-wealth economy on the foundation of the Main Street economy will require far more than adjustments at the margins. It will require a complete bottom-to-top redesign of our economic assumptions, values, and institutions.

Chapter 1, "Looking Upstream," spells out what it means to treat causes rather than symptoms and why getting our assumptions right is important.

Chapter 2, "Modern Alchemists and the Sport of Moneymaking," looks at the reality behind Wall Street's illusions and the variety of its methods for making money without the exertion of creating anything of real value in return.

Chapter 3, "A Real-Market Alternative," contrasts the Wall Street and Main Street economies and puts to rest the fallacy that the only alternative to rule by Wall Street capitalists is rule by communist bureaucrats.

Chapter 4, "More Than Tinkering at the Margins," spells out why the "adjustment at the margins" approach favored by establishment interests cannot stabilize the economy, reduce economic inequality, or prevent environmental collapse.

CHAPTER 1

>•◆•◆•◄

LOOKING UPSTREAM

A man was standing beside a stream when he saw a baby
struggling in the water. Without a thought he jumped in
and saved it. No sooner had he placed it gently on the shore
than he saw another and jumped in to save it, then another and another. Totally focused on saving babies, he never
thought to look upstream to answer the obvious question:
Where were the babies coming from, and how did they get
in the water?

ANONYMOUS

O ur economic system has failed in every dimension:
financial, environmental, and social. And the current
financial collapse provides an incontestable demonstration
that it has failed even on its own terms. Spending trillions of
dollars in an effort to restore this system to its previous condition is a reckless waste of time and resources and may be
the greatest misuse of federal government credit in history. The more intelligent course is to acknowledge the failure
and to set about redesigning our economic system from the
bottom up to align with the realities and opportunities of the
twenty-first century.

The Bush administration's strategy focused on bailing out
the Wall Street institutions that bore primary responsibility for creating the crisis; its hope was that if the government picked up enough of those institutions' losses and toxic
assets, they might decide to open the tap and get credit flowing again. The Obama administration has come into office

with a strong focus on economic stimulus, and particularly on green jobs—by far a more thoughtful and appropriate approach.

The real need, however, goes far beyond pumping new money into the economy to alleviate the consequences of the credit squeeze. We need to rebuild the system from the bottom up.

The recent credit meltdown has resulted in bailout commitments estimated in November 2008 to be $7.4 trillion, roughly half of the total U.S. gross domestic product (GDP).[1] Congressional passage the previous month of a $700 billion bailout package to be administered by the Treasury Department sparked a vigorous national debate that focused attention on the devastating consequences of Wall Street deregulation. Other, even larger government commitments, including $4.5 trillion from the Federal Reserve, largely escaped notice. I'll say more about this in chapter 7, "The High Cost of Phantom Wealth." Large as the bailouts were, the failure of the credit system is only one manifestation of a failed economy that is wildly out of balance with, and devastating to, both humans and the natural environment.

Wages are falling in the face of volatile food and energy prices. Consumer debt and housing foreclosures are setting historic records. The middle class is shrinking. The unconscionable and growing worldwide gap between rich and poor, with its related alienation, is eroding the social fabric to the point of fueling terrorism, genocide, and other violent criminal activity.

At the same time, excessive consumption is pushing Earth's ecosystems into collapse. Climate change and the related increase in droughts, floods, and wildfires are now recognized as serious threats. Scientists are in almost universal agreement that human activity bears substantial responsibility. We face severe water shortages, the erosion of topsoil, the loss of species, and the end of the fossil fuel subsidy. In each instance, a failed economic system that takes no account of the social and environmental costs of monetary profits bears major responsibility.

We face a monumental economic challenge that goes far beyond anything being discussed in the U.S. Congress or the corporate press. The hardships imposed by temporarily frozen credit markets pale in comparison to what lies ahead.

Even the significant funds that the Obama administration is committed to spending on economic stimulus will do nothing to address the deeper structural causes of our threefold financial, social, and environmental crisis. On the positive side, the financial crisis has put to rest the myths that our economic institutions are sound and that markets work best when deregulated. This creates an opportune moment to open a national conversation about what we can and must do to create an economic system that can work for all people for all time. *+ moral crises*

TREAT THE SYSTEM, NOT THE SYMPTOM

As a student in business school, I learned a basic rule of effective problem solving that has shaped much of my professional life. Our professors constantly admonished us to "look at the big picture." Treat the visible problem—a defective product or an underperforming employee—as the symptom of a deeper system failure. "Look upstream to find the root cause. Find the systemic cause and fix the system so the problem will not recur." That is one of the most important things I learned in more than twenty-six years of formal education.

Many years after I left academia, an observation by a wise Canadian friend and colleague, Tim Brodhead, reminded me of this lesson when he explained why most efforts fail to end poverty. "They stop at treating the symptoms of poverty, such as hunger and poor health, with food programs and clinics, without ever asking the obvious question: Why do a few people enjoy effortless abundance while billions of others who work far harder experience extreme deprivation?" He summed it up with this simple statement: "If you act to correct a problem without a theory about its cause, you inevitably treat only the symptoms." It is the same lesson my business professors were drumming into my brain many years earlier.

I was trained to apply this lesson within the confines of the business enterprise. Tim's observation made me realize that I had been applying it in my work as a development professional in Africa, Asia, and Latin America. For years I had been asking the question: What is the underlying cause of persistent poverty? Eventually, I came to realize that poverty is not the only significant unsolved human problem, and I enlarged the question to ask: Why is our economic system consigning billions of people to degrading poverty, destroying Earth's ecosystem, and tearing up the social fabric of civilized community? What must change if we are to have a world that works for all people and the whole of life?

Pleading with people to do the right thing is not going to get us where we need to go so long as we have a culture that celebrates the destructive behaviors we must now put behind us and as long as our institutions reward those behaviors. It is so much more sensible to direct our attention to making the right thing easy and pleasurable by working together to create a culture that celebrates positive values and to foster institutions that reward positive behavior.

WORSE THAN NO THEORY

What my wise colleague did not mention is that placing too much faith in a "bad" theory or story, one that offers incorrect explanations, may be even worse than acting with no theory at all. A bad theory can lead us to false solutions that amplify the actions that caused the problem in the first place. Indeed, a bad theory or story can lead whole societies to persist in self-destructive behavior to the point of self-extinction.

The cultural historian Jared Diamond tells of the Viking colony on the coast of Greenland that perished of hunger next to waters abundant with fish; it had a cultural theory, or

PHANTOM WEALTH

Also called illusory wealth, this is wealth that appears or disappears as if by magic. The term generally denotes money created by accounting entries or the inflation of asset bubbles unrelated to the creation of anything of real value or utility. The high-tech-stock and housing bubbles are examples.

Phantom wealth also includes financial assets created by debt pyramids in which financial institutions engage in complex trading and lending schemes based on fictitious or overvalued assets in order to generate phantom profits and justify outsized management fees. Debt pyramids may be used as a device to feed financial bubbles, as in the subprime mortgage scam.

Those engaged in creating phantom wealth collect handsome "performance" fees for their services at each step and walk away with their gains. When borrowers begin to default on debts they cannot pay, the bubble bursts and the debt pyramid collapses.

Those who had no part in creating or profiting from the scam are then left to absorb the losses and to sort out the phantom-wealth claims still held by the perpetrators against the marketable real wealth of the larger society. It is all legal, which makes it a perfect crime.

REAL WEALTH

Real wealth has intrinsic, as contrasted to exchange, value. Life, not money, is the measure of real-wealth value.

The most important forms are beyond price and are unavailable for market purchase. These include healthy, happy children, loving families, caring communities, and a beautiful, healthy, natural environment.

Real wealth also includes all the many things of intrinsic artistic, spiritual, or utilitarian value essential to maintaining the various forms of living wealth. These may or may not have a market price. They include healthful food, fertile land, pure water, clean air, caring relationships and loving parents, education, health care, fulfilling opportunities for service, and time for meditation and spiritual reflection.

Because of the essential role of caring relationships, the monetization or commodification of real wealth, which generally translates into the monetization or commodification of relationships, tends to diminish its real value. Examples include replacing parental caregivers with paid child care workers.

In contrast to a phantom-wealth economy, money in a real-wealth economy is not used as a measure or a storehouse of value, but solely as a convenient medium of exchange. A phantom-wealth economy seeks to monetize and commodify relationships to increase dependence on money; a real-wealth economy favors relationships based on mutual caring that reduce dependence on money.

story, that eating fish was not "civilized."[2] On a much larger scale, the human future is now in question and the cause can be traced, in part, to economic theories that serve the narrow interests of a few and result in devastating consequences for all.

As we are perplexed by the behavior of the Vikings who perished because of their unwillingness to give up an obviously foolish theory, so future generations may be perplexed by our foolish embrace of some absurd theories of our own, including the theory that financial speculation and the inflation of financial bubbles create real wealth and make us richer. No need to be concerned that we are trashing Earth's life support system and destroying the social bonds of family and community, because eventually, or so the theory goes, we will have enough money to heal the environment and end poverty.

This theory led to economic policies that for decades served to create a mirage of phantom wealth that vanished before our eyes as the subprime mortgage crisis unfolded. Even with this dramatic demonstration that we were chasing a phantom, most observers have yet to acknowledge that the financial speculation was not creating wealth at all. Rather, it was merely increasing the claims of financial speculators on the shrinking pool of everyone else's real wealth.

A NEW STORY FOR A NEW ECONOMY

A theory, of course, is nothing more than a fancy name for a story that presumes to explain how things work. It is now commonly acknowledged that we humans are on a course to self-destruction. Climate chaos, the end of cheap oil, collapsing fisheries, dead rivers, falling water tables, terrorism, genocidal wars, financial collapse, species extinction, thirty thousand child deaths daily from poverty—and in the richest country in the world, millions squeezed out of the middle class—are all evidence of the monumental failure of our existing cultural stories and the institutions to which they give rise. We have good reason to fear for our future.

At first, each of the many disasters that confront us appears distinct. In fact, they all have a common origin that our feeble "solutions" fail to address for lack of an adequate theory. *Agenda for a New Economy* is a big-picture story, or theory, of where we went wrong in the design of our economic institutions and what we can do about it. We do, in fact, have the means to create an economy that fulfills six criteria of economic health. Such an economy would

1. provide everyone with the opportunity for a healthy, dignified, and fulfilling life.

2. bring human consumption into balance with Earth's natural systems.

3. nurture relationships within strong, caring communities.

4. honor sound, rule-based market principles.

5. support an equitable and socially efficient allocation of resources.

6. fulfill the democratic ideal of one-person, one-vote citizen sovereignty.

A BOOK FOR THOSE READY TO LOOK UPSTREAM

Agenda for a New Economy is a book for people who are looking upstream, not to place blame, but to find real solutions to the system failure that now threatens our future. At its core, it is about the cultural stories that shape our collective values and the institutional systems that shape our relationships with one another and with Earth. The relevance is global, but the primary focus is on the United States because U.S. economic values and institutions are somewhat distinctive and have a powerful global influence

The justified public outrage against the breathtaking excesses of Wall Street creates an opportunity to mobilize political support for a new economy that shifts our economic priorities from making money for rich people to creating better lives for all and that reallocates our economic resources from destructive, or merely wasteful, uses to beneficial ones. Our present Wall Street–dominated system is very effective at doing exactly what it is designed to do. To get a different outcome, we need a different design grounded in different values and a different understanding of wealth, our human nature, and the sources of human happiness and well-being. The basic design elements of the New Economy we seek are known, as I will elaborate in subsequent chapters.

We face an urgent need for a national and international discourse on economic policy choices that lead to a bottom-to-top structural transformation of the economy in order to strengthen community and reallocate resources to where they best serve. I have written *Agenda for a New Economy* as a contribution to this discourse. I hope you will be encouraged to engage your friends, colleagues, community, and media contacts in discussion about the foundational economic policy choices at hand and will find this book a useful tool.

CHAPTER 2

>•◆•◆•◄

MODERN ALCHEMISTS AND THE SPORT OF MONEYMAKING

The capitalist ideal is to create money out of nothing, without a need to produce anything of real value in return. Wall Street has turned this ideal into a high-stakes competitive sport. Money is the means of scoring, and *Forbes* magazine is the unofficial scorekeeper issuing periodic reports on the "richest people" ranked in the order of their total financial assets. The player with the most assets wins. Because the scoring is competitive, no player has "enough" money so long as another player in the game has more.

Making money with no effort can be an addictive experience. I recall my excitement back in the mid-'60s, when Fran, my wife, and I first made a modest investment in a mutual fund and watched our savings grow magically by hundreds and then thousands of dollars with no effort whatever on our part. We felt as if we had discovered the philosopher's stone that turned cheap metals into gold. We got a case of Wall Street fever on what by current standards was a tiny scale.

Of course, most of what we call magic is illusion. When the credit collapse pulled back the curtain to expose Wall Street's inner workings, all the world was able to see the extent to which Wall Street is a world of deception, misrepresentation, and insider dealing in the business of creating phantom wealth without a corresponding contribution to the creation of anything of real value. It was such an ugly picture that Wall Street's seriously corrupted institutions stopped lending even to each other for the very good reason they didn't trust anyone's financial statements.

PHANTOM WEALTH

In business school, I learned the art of assessing investment options to maximize financial return. My teachers never mentioned that what we were really learning was to maximize returns to people who had money, that is, to make rich people richer. Nor did they mention that if pursued mechanically, the methods we were learning might result in the creation of phantom wealth. That concept didn't exist.

Buried in the details of our calculations, no one asked, What is money? Why should we assume that maximizing financial return maximizes the creation of real value? I don't recall whether such questions ever occurred to me. If they did, I kept them to myself for fear of being dismissed as hopelessly stupid.

Nor did our teachers ever point out, perhaps because they didn't recognize it themselves, that money is only an accounting chit with no intrinsic existence or value outside the human mind. Certainly, they never told us that money is a system of power and that the more dependent we are on money as the mediator of human relationships, the more readily those who have the power to create money and to decide who gets it can abuse that power.

If we had been paying close attention, we might have noticed that many fortunes were the result of financial speculation, fraud, government subsidies, the sale of harmful products, and the abuse of monopoly power. But this was rarely mentioned.

PHANTOM-WEALTH EXUBERANCE

The illusions of Wall Street are captured in the titles and publication dates of popular books such as:

Dow 36,000: The New Strategy for Profiting from the Coming Rise in the Stock Market (2000)

Dow 30,000 by 2008: Why It's Different This Time (2004)

Why the Real Estate Boom Will Not Bust (2006)

It is easy to confuse money with the real wealth for which it can be exchanged—our labor, ideas, land, gold, health care, food, and all the other things with value in their own right. The illusions of phantom wealth are so convincing that most Wall Street players believe the wealth they are creating is real. They are standing so far upstream, they may never see the babies floating downstream, which the system they serve is throwing into the water.

The market, of course, makes no distinction between the dollars acquired through means that enriched society, those created by means that impoverished society, and those simply created out of thin air. Money is money, and the more you have, the more the market eagerly responds to your every whim. To believe that paper or electronic money is real wealth, rather than simply a coupon that may be redeemed for goods and services of real intrinsic value, confuses illusion with reality.

 Those who create phantom wealth, and those who are the beneficiaries of mutual funds or retirement funds invested in phantom wealth, may never realize that they are giving its holder a claim on the real wealth produced by others, and that phantom-wealth dollars created out of nothing dilute the claims of everyone else to the available stock of real wealth.

They may also fail to realize that Wall Street and its international counterparts have created phantom-wealth claims far in excess of the value of all the world's real wealth, creating expectations of future security and comforts that can never be fulfilled.

The Edmunds Fallacy

While doing the research in 1997 for *The Post-Corporate World: Life after Capitalism,* I read an article in *Foreign Policy* by John Edmunds, then a finance professor at Babson College and the Arthur D. Little School of Management, titled "Securities: The New Wealth Machine." Given that *Foreign Policy* is a highly respected professional journal, I was surprised an article based on such obviously flawed logic had made it through its editorial review process. The following is an excerpt:

Securitization—the issuance of high-quality bonds and stocks—has become the most powerful engine of wealth creation in today's world economy. Financial securities have grown to the point that they are now worth more than a year's worldwide output of goods and services, and soon they will be worth more than two years' output. While politicians concentrate on trade balances and intellectual property rights, these financial instruments are the leading component of wealth today as well as its fastest-growing generator.

Historically, manufacturing, exporting, and direct investment produced prosperity through income creation. Wealth was created when a portion of income was diverted from consumption into investment in buildings, machinery, and technological change. Societies accumulated wealth slowly over generations. Now many societies, and indeed the entire world, have learned how to create wealth directly. The new approach requires that a state find ways to increase the *market value* of its stock of productive assets. [Emphasis in the original.] . . . Wealth is also created when money, foreign or domestic, flows into the capital market of a country and raises the value of its quoted securities. . . .

Nowadays, wealth is created when the managers of a business enterprise give high priority to rewarding the shareholders and bondholders. The greater the rewards, the more the shares and bonds are likely to be worth in the financial markets. . . . An economic policy that aims to achieve growth by wealth creation therefore does not attempt to increase the production of goods and services, except as a secondary objective.[1]

Professor Edmunds is telling government policymakers that they should no longer concern themselves with producing real wealth by increasing the national output of goods and services that have real utility. They should put all that aside. They can grow their national economies faster with less exertion by securitizing real assets so that investors can put them into play in financial markets and pump up their value to create gigantic asset bubbles.

Rarely have I come across such a clear example of the widespread belief, seemingly pervasive on Wall Street, that inflating asset bubbles creates real wealth. Apparently, even the editors of *Foreign Policy* and their editorial reviewers failed to recognize what I'll call the "Edmunds fallacy" for the sake of giving it a shorthand name. Asset bubbles create only phantom wealth that increases the claims of the holder to a society's real wealth and thereby dilutes the claims of everyone else. Edmunds did not invent this fallacy, but his *Foreign Policy* article lent it new intellectual respectability and, as noted below, apparently stirred the imagination of Wall Street insiders.

THE POLICY PREFERENCE FOR PHANTOM WEALTH

In recent decades, the Federal Reserve has allied with the U.S. Treasury Department and Wall Street banks to give the creation of phantom wealth priority over the production of real wealth. Rather than attempt to dampen asset bubbles like the tech-stock bubble of the 1990s and the housing bubble of 2000s, the Fed pursued cheap money policies to encourage borrowing by speculators to support continuing inflation. The growing power and profits of Wall Street signaled the success of these policies.

Meanwhile, the U.S. industrial sector was decimated as production was outsourced to low-wage economies to increase share prices. In many cases, Wall Street inflated the stock prices of its favored companies, which then gave them the power to buy up other companies. Its highly valued stocks allowed WorldCom, for example, to purchase MCI and a dozen other companies. Later the market turned down, and WorldCom was forced into bankruptcy. Stock bubbles create major market disruptions.

The subprime mortgage boom was built on creating overvalued assets that served as collateral for more borrowing to create more overvalued assets. Federal bailouts to save overleveraged financial institutions when the bubble bursts represent another resource allocation distortion.

Reading the Edmunds article reminded me of a conversation I'd had some years earlier with Malaysia's minister of forestry. He told me in all seriousness that Malaysia would be better off once all its trees were cut down and the proceeds were deposited in interest-bearing accounts, because interest grows faster than trees. An image flashed into my mind of a barren and lifeless Malaysian landscape populated only by banks, their computers happily whirring away, calculating the interest on those deposits. This is exactly the kind of disaster to which the Edmunds fallacy leads.

In his 2008 book *Bad Money,* the journalist and former Republican Party political strategist Kevin Phillips notes that the Edmunds article was widely discussed on Wall Street and implies that it may have inspired the securitization of housing mortgages.[2] If it did, that would make it one of history's most influential academic papers.

No matter who or what inspired the securitization of housing mortgages, Edmunds's logic is the underlying logic of Wall Street. Forget production and the interests of working people, communities, and nature. Focus on driving up the market price of financial securities by whatever means. The subprime mortgage debacle was a hugely costly test of a badly flawed theory.

Securitizing Subprime Mortgages

After the terrorist attacks of September 11, 2001, the U.S. Federal Reserve sought to counteract the resulting economic disruption by lowering interest rates. By July 2003, they were down to 1 percent, which was below the rate of inflation. The negative cost of borrowing set off a housing bubble and an orgy of leveraged buyouts. Wall Street investment banks invented creative instruments that justified the collection of fees for themselves, allowed them to pass the risks to others, and kept their positions in what came to be called "toxic assets" off their own books.

The availability of cheap mortgages stimulated the housing market, which in turn inflated housing prices. The faster the bubble of easy profits grew, the faster new money flowed in to inflate it even more. Pundits and politicians, embracing the Edmunds fallacy, celebrated the expansion of homeownership and the creation of what was mostly phantom wealth.

Banks enlisted independent brokers to sign up borrowers, on commission. The banks bundled the mortgages into securities they sold to investment banks that packaged them into more complex securities and in turn sold them to hedge funds whose math wizards packaged them into even more complex securities that no one really understood.

These securities were "insured" against loss by other highly leveraged Wall Street institutions, like AIG, which pocketed the premiums but kept only minimal reserves to cover potential losses on the theory that housing prices could only go up. The investment banks and hedge funds that created the securities claimed the insurance eliminated the risk of holding such securities and hired ratings agencies to certify their claims. The securities were then sold to pension funds, endowment funds, mutual funds, and others as high-yield, risk-free investments. The players at each step along the way made a fortune from the collection of fees and commissions while passing the risks on to the next guy.[3]

In the home mortgage industry of an earlier time, local banks made loans to local borrowers and carried the risk on their books. If a homeowner could not meet the mortgage payments, the bank that made the loan bore the loss. This encouraged a careful review of mortgage applications to assure the financial solvency of the borrower.

In the "modernized" financial system, the bank captures a fee for signing up the borrower. Since the risk associated with a potential default is passed to others, the bank has no incentive to exercise due diligence, an obvious system design flaw. According to the famed international financier George Soros, "Credit standards collapsed, and mortgages were made widely available to people with low credit ratings. [Thus the term *subprime mortgage*.] . . . 'Alt-A' (or liar loans), with low or no documentation, were common, including, at the extreme, 'ninja' loans (no job, no income, no assets), frequently with the active connivance of the mortgage brokers and mortgage lenders."[4] The norm was clear. Just get a signature on a mortgage document and collect the fee. The bigger the loan, the better. No worry if the borrower can't pay. That will be the next guy's problem.

Of course, if worst came to worst, the government could likely be pressured into a bailout by the threat that if it didn't pick up the losses, banks would stop making loans and the economy would collapse.

The details of what happened are far more complex than what I've outlined here, but that is the essence. When obviously unqualified borrowers defaulted, the whole house of cards began tumbling down and the phantom wealth that Wall Street had created through mortgage securitization disappeared even more rapidly than it had magically appeared—as did the trillions of dollars of government bailout money that followed.

A Bubble Is Just a Bubble

Contrary to Edmunds's "logic," an asset bubble, real estate or otherwise, does not create wealth. A rise in the market price of a house from $200,000 to $400,000 does not make it more functional or comfortable. The real consequence of a real estate bubble is to increase the financial power of those who own property relative to those who do not. Wall Street encouraged homeowners to monetize their market gains with mortgages, which it then converted into securities and sold off to the unwary, including the pension funds that many homeowners counted on for their retirement.

When the housing bubble inevitably burst, dazed homeowners walked away, many in financial ruin, from properties on which they owed more than the market value. Securities based on these mortgages lost value, and the overleveraged Wall Street players could not meet their financial commitments. In the face of escalating defaults, the whole system of interlocking credit obligations collapsed, and Wall Street turned to taxpayers for a bailout, warning that unless the government made it whole, credit would dry up and the whole economy would collapse for lack of money.

Whether the alarming announcement by the banks was more threat than warning, we may never know, but it was surely effective. The government responded with trillions of dollars in public bailout money. The recipient institutions held extravagant parties, paid out executive bonuses and dividends, and financed acquisitions. The bailout money seemed to vanish as quickly as the phantom wealth of the housing bubble. Credit, however, remained frozen for reasons yet to be explained.

Debt Slaves to Wall Street

Why do we tolerate Wall Street's reckless excess and abuse of power? In part, it is because so many people of influence have bought into the Edmunds fallacy. Many actively celebrate the Wall Street production of phantom wealth and our growing reliance on other countries to produce the goods and services we consume. By the prevailing story, we, the United States, serve the global economy by specializing in making money and consuming the goods that others produce. In the fantasy world of Wall Street, this all makes perfect sense.

If you have difficulty understanding the Wall Street logic,

which is taught in many economics and finance courses, it may be because you are in touch with reality. No matter what Wall Street says, a bad loan is still a bad loan no matter how many times it has been sliced, diced, and repackaged into ever more complex derivatives certified by Standard & Poor's as AAA.

Even more, however, we tolerate Wall Street and rush to bail it out because it controls the issuance of credit and thereby our access to money in a world that has made us dependent on money for almost every aspect of our lives. Here is a simple description of how the money-creation process works.

✳ ALCHEMISTS IN EYESHADES

Most people think of accounting as a rather boring subject, but pay attention here, because nearly every dollar in circulation has been created by a private bank with a deceptively simple accounting sleight-of-hand. Understand how it works, and you understand why our current system of debt money created by private banks for private gain makes it possible for a few people to acquire obscene amounts of unearned money while sticking the rest of us with the bill.

My college economics professor taught us that banks are financial intermediaries between savers and borrowers: A saver makes a deposit, and the bank lends that money to a borrower to finance a business or home. But that isn't the way it really works.

Unless you are holding a long-term certificate of deposit, you have immediate access to the money you deposit in your bank. If you borrow money from the bank, you also have immediate access to the funds in the account that the bank created in your name when it made the loan. When a loan is issued, the bank's accountant enters two numbers in the bank's accounting records: She records the borrower's promise to repay the loan as an asset, and the money the bank puts into the borrower's account as a liability.

At first glance, it looks like these entries cancel each other out, which in a sense is true. The key is that neither entry existed previously. With the accountant's entries, the bank created new money from nothing in the amount of the loan principal and caused the amount of money in the economy as a whole to increase. At the same time, the borrower acquired a legal obligation to repay the principal with interest.

This, in fact, is how all money (except for coins and some special notes) is created. It should be noted that the bank-created money is purely electronic. There isn't even a paper record. You might say it has no existence outside the human mind.

Needless to say, granting banks the right to create money with a computer keystroke and then lend it out at interest makes banking very profitable, and Wall Street, which owns the banks, enormously powerful. It also contributes to financial instability and inequality, creates an economic growth imperative, and distorts economic priorities, all costs to society I explain in chapter 7, "The High Cost of Phantom Wealth." The damage is increased by orders of magnitude when banks discover the profit potential in putting this money-creation power at the service of financial speculators and predators engaged in the creation of phantom wealth.

▶•◆•◆•◀

Wall Street, as economic system or syndicate, is extremely good at what it is designed and managed to do: make a few people fabulously wealthy without the exertion and distraction of producing anything of real value. From the perspective of the beneficiaries, money is money, and those who have lots of it can indulge themselves in luxuries beyond the imagination of the kings and emperors of previous times. The major failing of the existing financial system from the perspective of its Wall Street beneficiaries is the tendency for asset bubbles to collapse and wipe out large portions of their asset statements, even forcing them to sell off estates, yachts, and private jets at fire-sale prices.

When the bubbles are growing, Wall Street's gain is a net loss for the rest of the society. The costs fall on those who don't have the money to live in splendid isolation from the social and environmental realities of our troubled planet. The idea that economic growth will solve this problem has no substance, because the so-called rising tide lifts only the yachts and swamps the desperate, naked swimmers. It works out fine for the winners that growth in Wall Street financial assets plays out for the rest of society as growing inequality. What is a wealthy class without a servant class?

There is an alternative to Wall Street phantom-wealth capitalism: a real-market economy.

CHAPTER 3

►•◆•◆•◄

A REAL-MARKET
ALTERNATIVE

We have long been told that the only alternative to the rapacious excess of capitalism is the debilitating repression of communism. This sets up a false and dangerously self-limiting choice between two extremes, both of which failed because they created a concentration of unaccountable power that stifled liberty and creativity for all but the few at the top.

The alternative to both of these discredited experiments in centralized power is an economic system that roots power in people and communities of place and that unleashes our innate human capacities for cooperation and creativity. We have a historic opportunity to bring such an economy into being. The key is the often mentioned distinction between our existing Wall Street and Main Street economies.

WALL STREET VERSUS MAIN STREET

Wall Street and *Main Street* are names given to two economies with strikingly different priorities, values, and institutions. They are distinct but interconnected, and they are often in competition.

Wall Street

Wall Street refers to the institutions of big finance and the captive corporations that serve them. They may be located anywhere, not necessarily on the famous street in New York City that has become a global symbol of capitalism.

Wall Street is a world of pure finance in the business of using money to make money by whatever means for people who have money. It has perfected the arts of financial speculation, corporate asset stripping, predatory lending, risk shifting, leveraging, and creating debt pyramids. Maximizing financial return is the name of the game. Successful players are rewarded with celebrity, extravagant perks, and vast financial fortunes.

Wall Street players may justify their actions with the claim that they are creating wealth for the larger benefit of the society, a convenient bit of self-delusion. Money isn't wealth. It is only an accounting chit, a number of value only because by social convention we are willing to accept it in return for things of real value. It has no inherent value or existence outside the human mind.

Main Street

Main Street is the world of local businesses and working people engaged in producing real goods and services to provide a livelihood for themselves, their families, and communities. Main Street is more varied in its priorities, values, and institutions. Like the diverse species of a healthy ecosystem, its enterprises take many forms, from sole proprietorships and family businesses to cooperatives and locally owned and rooted privately held corporations. Achieving a positive financial return is an essential condition of staying in business, but most Main Street businesses function within a framework of community values and interests that moderate the drive for profit.

I grew up in a small town in which my family had a successful retail music and appliance business. My dad took great pride in standing behind and servicing everything he sold. I recall the not infrequent experience of his answering the phone during dinner and asking Mother to keep his dinner warm as he got up to open the store for a customer with an urgent need. One, I remember, was from a local musician who had broken his guitar pick and needed a replacement for a job he was playing that night. At that time, a pick was probably no more than a 10-cent item.

I understood that business was a service to the community and that that was what businesspeople provided. Many Main Street business owners continue to this day to embrace a similar commitment to community service, including the twenty thousand members of the Business Alliance for Local Living Economies already engaged in building the New Economy. This commitment is an essential part of what distinguishes Main Street from Wall Street.

CORPORATIONS

So what of corporations? Many of them produce beneficial goods and services that we need in our daily lives. Where do they fit between Wall Street and Main Street? The answer is, "It depends."

The legal form of the publicly traded limited liability corporation was invented a bit more than four hundred years ago when the king of England issued a charter to the East India Company. He thereby granted a group of investors, including himself, an exclusive crown-protected license to colonize the lands of Asia and expropriate their resources through trade and military force.

The corporate charter suits this purpose well: It creates the legal capacity to amass under unified management the power of virtually unlimited financial capital; moreover, the shareholders who benefit are exempted from liability for the consequences of management's actions beyond the amount of their investment. It is an open invitation to abuse to which even saints are prone to succumb.

That said, there are incorporated businesses with identifiable responsible owners who live in the communities in which their businesses are located and who operate their corporations as responsible members of their community. These corporations are properly considered part of the Main Street economy.

Once a corporation sells its shares publicly through Wall Street exchanges or to Wall Street private equity investors, however, it becomes an agent of Wall Street. Whatever values it may have had before are, in all probability, subordinated to Wall Street interests and values. The production of goods and services becomes purely incidental to the primary business purpose of making money. As a onetime executive of the Odwalla corporation told me, "So long as we were privately owned by the founders, we were in the business of producing and marketing healthful fruit juice products. Once we went public, everything changed. From that event forward, we were in the business of making money."

Notwithstanding the title of my first book on the global economy, *When Corporations Rule the World,* the real economic power in this country resides with Wall Street institutions that buy and sell major corporations as if they were mere commodities. Any chief executive officer of a Wall Street–traded corporation that puts social or environmental considerations ahead of financial return will soon find himself cast out in disgrace through a revolt of institutional shareholders or a hostile takeover.

Visit a contemporary corporate headquarters and you see people, buildings, furnishings, and office equipment. By all appearances, the people are running things. An organizational chart will show clear lines of authority leading to a CEO who in turn reports to a board of directors. It is easy to think of a corporation as a community of people. That is, however, a misleading characterization, because the people are all employees of the corporation and paid to serve its financial interests. If the corporation is Wall Street owned, they are bound to serve Wall Street interests, and their employment is solely at Wall Street's pleasure.

The publicly traded limited liability corporation is more accurately described as a pool of money with special legal rights and protections. Even the CEO and directors can be dismissed without notice or recourse. In theory, it is the shareholders whom management serves; however, since most shares are held in trust by various institutional investors, the real shareholders are generally invisible even to the corporate officers.

In effect, management is hired by money to nurture money's growth and reproduction in disregard of all other considerations. The result is a global capitalist economy destructive of both life and the human soul.

THE MARKET ALTERNATIVE

Defenders of capitalist excess insist that capitalism is synonymous with markets and private ownership. If not entirely false, this claim is at best seriously misleading, and it obscures our ability to see an obvious nonrepressive alternative.

The theory of the market economy traces back to the eighteenth-century Scottish economist Adam Smith and the publication in 1776 of his *Inquiry into the Nature and Causes of the Wealth of Nations*. Considered by many to be the most influential economics book ever written, Smith's seminal text articulates the powerful and wonderfully democratic ideal of a self-organizing economy that creates an equitable and socially optimal allocation of society's productive resources through the interaction of small buyers and sellers making decisions based on their individual needs, interests, and abilities.

Market theory, as articulated by Smith and those who subsequently elaborated on his ideas, developed into an elegant and coherent intellectual construction grounded in carefully articulated assumptions regarding the conditions under which such self-organizing processes would indeed lead to socially optimal outcomes. Market fundamentalists generally ignore the essential conditions, which include:

- Buyers and sellers must be too small to influence the market price.

FREEDOM TO COMMIT FRAUD

The term *free market* is a code word for an unregulated market that allows the rich to consume and monopolize resources for personal gain free from accountability for the broader social and environmental consequences. A free market rewards financial rogues and speculators who profit from governmental, social, and environmental subsidies, speculation, the abuse of monopoly power, and financial fraud, creating an open and often irresistible invitation to externalize costs and increase inequality.

Markets work best within the framework of a caring community. The stronger the relations of mutual trust and caring, the more the market becomes self-policing. The need for formal governmental oversight and intervention is minimal. An economy of powerful corporations governed by a culture of greed and a belief that it is their legal duty to maximize returns to shareholders is quite a different matter and is difficult for even the strongest governments to control.

- Complete information must be available to all participants, and there can be no trade secrets.

- Sellers must bear the full cost of the products they sell and incorporate them into the sale price.

- Investment capital must remain within national borders, and trade between countries must be balanced.

- Savings must be invested in the creation of productive capital rather than in speculative trading.

As you have probably noticed, this doesn't look much like Wall Street. Although not a perfect match, it looks a good deal more like Main Street.

Historians have traced the origin of the term *capitalism* to the mid-1800s, long after Adam Smith's death. It referred to an economic and social regime in which the ownership and benefits of capital are appropriated by the few to the exclusion of the many who through their labor make capital productive.[1] This, of course, describes with considerable precision the characteristics of Wall Street.

CAPITALISM CLOAKED IN MARKET RHETORIC

Capitalism's claim to the mantle of the market has no more substance than the claim of the rogue in the tale of "The Emperor's New Clothes," who declared that he had cloaked the ruler in a fine gown. In selectively culling bits and pieces of market theory to argue that the public interest is best served by giving globe-spanning megacorporations a license to maximize their profits without public restraint, capitalism has distorted market theory beyond recognition to legitimize an ideology without logical or empirical foundation in the service of a narrow class interest.

Wearing the mantle of the market, capitalism's agents

Are capitalism as it has come to operate + sustainability antithetical

vigorously advance public policies that create conditions diametrically opposed to those required for markets to function in a socially optimal way. Table 3.1 provides an overview of some of the major differences between the Wall Street capitalist economy we have and the kind of Main Street market economy we need to encourage.

Like cancer cells that attempt to hide from the body's immune system by masking themselves as healthy cells, capitalism's agents attempt to conceal themselves from society's immune system by masquerading as agents of a healthy market economy. Capitalism has become so skilled in this deception that we now find our economic and political leaders committed to policies that serve the pathology at the expense of the healthy body. To restore health we must recognize the diseased cells for what they are and either surgically remove them or deprive them of access to the body's nutrients.

Under a socialist system, government consolidates power unto itself. Under a capitalist model, government falls captive to corporate interests and facilitates the consolidation of corporate power. In a true market system, democratically accountable governments provide an appropriate framework of rules within which people, communities, entrepreneurs, and responsible investors self-organize in predominantly local markets to meet their economic needs in socially and environmentally responsible ways.

▶•◆•◆•◀

In the Wall Street economy, money is both means and end, and the primary product is phantom wealth—money disconnected from the production or possession of anything of real value. The Main Street economy is largely engaged in creating real wealth from real resources to meet real needs. Wall Street is very good at making rich people richer, but it has no concern for the health of people, community, or nature except as sources of short-term profit.

Table 3.1 Wall Street Capitalism versus Main Street Markets

	Wall Street capitalism	Main Street markets
Dominant driver	Making money	Creating livelihoods
Defining activity	Using money to make money for those who have money	Employing available resources to meet the needs of the community
Firm size	Very large	Small and medium
Costs	Externalized to the public	Internalized by the user
Ownership	Impersonal and absentee	Personal and rooted
Financial capital	Global with no borders	Local/national with clear borders
Purpose of investment	Maximize private profit	Increase beneficial output
The role of profit	An end to be maximized	A means to sustain viability
Efficiency measure	Returns to financial capital	Returns to living capital
Coordinating mechanisms	Central planning by mega-corporations	Self-organizing markets and networks
Cooperation	Can occur among competitors to escape the discipline of competition	Occurs among people and communities to advance the common good
Purpose of competition	Eliminates the unfit	Stimulates efficiency and innovation
Government role	Protect the interests of property	Advance the human interest
Trade	Free and unregulated	Fair and balanced
Political orientation	A democracy of dollars	A democracy of persons

Draw back the curtain, as the credit collapse has done, to reveal the inner workings of Wall Street, and it begins to look less like a legitimate business enterprise and more like a criminal syndicate running a lucrative extortion racket. The nearest equivalent in nature is a cancer that drains the body's energy but produces nothing useful in return. You don't "fix" a cancer; you excise it and rebuild the healthy tissue. Main Street is the healthy tissue and the foundation of the New Economy.

CHAPTER 4

>•◆•◆•◀

MORE THAN TINKERING
AT THE MARGINS

When economic failure is systemic, temporary fixes, even very expensive ones like the Wall Street bailout, are like putting a bandage on a cancer. They may create a temporary sense of confidence, but the effect is solely cosmetic.

IT'S OVER

Appropriate and effective action needs to begin with a recognition that we can no longer organize our economic life in the ways to which we have become accustomed. They cannot be restored more than momentarily, no matter how committed and sophisticated our bailout and stimulus plans, because we have already passed the limits of stress that our economic, environmental, and social systems will tolerate.

"Solutions" that do not take this basic reality into account not only are doomed to fail but also are likely to accelerate an environmental and social collapse. We must act decisively to actualize a vision of possibility appropriate to the reality of our situation.

Unfortunately, even influential pundits who recognize the seriousness of the environmental and social dimensions of the current economic crisis generally limit their recommendations to a tune-up of the existing system. Rare indeed are establishment voices calling for a redesign of our economic institutions.

Jeffrey Sachs and James Gustave Speth are both influential establishment authors who in their most recent books present nearly identical statements of the need for action to reverse environmental damage and eliminate poverty. Their recommendations, however, are worlds apart. Sachs focuses on the symptoms and prescribes a bandage. Speth takes a holistic approach and prescribes a cultural and institutional transformation.[1]

In Table 4.1 I contrast the perspectives of Sachs and Speth on three defining economic issues. The differences are instructive, because we must learn to distinguish those who would lull us into believing we can get by with adjustments at the margins, à la Sachs, the neoclassical economist, from those who offer serious solutions based on a deep system redesign, à la Speth, the systems ecologist.

SACHS: PAINLESS FINE-TUNING

Jeffrey Sachs, an economist by training and perspective, is known for his work as an economic adviser to national governments and an array of public institutions. The *New York Times* once described him as "probably the most important economist in the world."[2]

Sachs opens his most recent book, *Common Wealth: Economics for a Crowded Planet* (2008), with a powerful and unequivocal problem statement that raises expectations of a bold break with the economic orthodoxy of those he refers to as "free-market ideologues."

> The challenges of sustainable development—protecting the environment, stabilizing the world's population, narrowing the gaps between rich and poor, and ending extreme poverty—will take center stage. Global cooperation will have to come to the fore. The very idea of competing nation-states that scramble for markets,

Table 4.1 Tinkering versus Transforming

	Marginal adjustment (Sachs)	System redesign (Speth)
Economic growth	Growth in GDP is a valid measure of human progress, prosperity, and increased well-being. More is generally better. Given a combination of market forces, the provision of public incentives, and a proper mix of technology, there is no inherent environmental limit to economic growth.	Economic growth is disrupting the values and living systems essential to human well-being. Beyond a minimal threshold of consumption, building community, rather than increasing the consumption of stuff, is the key to increasing human health and happiness.
Equity	Poverty, not equity, is the issue, and the proper response is to kick-start the growth process within the world's remaining pockets of absolute poverty by introducing technologies and social services funded by foreign aid.	Extreme poverty is the inevitable other side of the coin of extreme wealth and can be resolved only through redistribution from those who have more than they need to those who have less.
Governing system	The institutions of capitalism as currently constituted can resolve environmental and social problems through a combination of voluntary action, modest public expenditure, and fine-tuning at the margins.	The operating systems of capitalism must be fundamentally redesigned to internalize costs, distribute ownership, and establish accountability for the human and natural consequences of economic decisions.

power, and resources will become passé. . . . The pressures of scarce energy resources, growing environmental stresses, a rising global population, legal and illegal mass migration, shifting economic power, and vast

inequalities of income are too great to be left to naked
market forces and untrammeled geopolitical competition among nations.[3]

This statement would have served equally well as an opening
statement for Speth, who agrees that government must play
an essential role, and nations must cooperate, in any effort to
effect a meaningful solution. From there, however, we might
wonder whether they live in different worlds.

The Tech Fix

Sachs assures us that we can end environmental stress and
poverty with modest investments in existing technologies to
sequester carbon, develop new energy sources, end population growth, make more efficient use of water and other natural resources, and jump-start economic growth in the world's
remaining pockets of persistent poverty. In a 2007 lecture to
the Royal Society in London, Sachs made clear his belief that
there is no need to redistribute wealth, cut back material consumption, or otherwise reorganize the economy.

> I do not believe that the solution to this problem is a
> massive cutback of our consumption levels or our liv-
> ing standards. I think the solution is smarter living. I do
> believe that technology is absolutely critical, and I do
> not believe . . . that the essence of the problem is that we
> face a zero sum that must be redistributed. I'm going to
> argue that there's a way for us to use the knowledge that
> we have, the technology that we have, to make broad
> progress in material conditions, to not require or ask the
> rich to take sharp cuts of living standards, but rather to
> live with smarter technologies that are sustainable, and
> thereby to find a way for the rest of the world, which
> yearns for it, and deserves it as far as I'm concerned, to

raise their own material conditions as well. The costs
are much less than people think.[4]

Far from calling for a restraint on consumption, Sachs projects global economic expansion from $60 trillion in 2005
to $420 trillion in 2050. Relying on what he calls a "back-
of-the-envelope calculation," he estimates that the world's
wealthy nations can eliminate extreme poverty and develop
and apply the necessary technologies to address environmental needs with an expenditure of a mere 2.4 percent of the
projected midcentury economic output. Problem painlessly
solved, at least in Sachs's mind.

Growth as Usual

Sachs gives no indication of why, if we can stabilize population and meet the needs of the poor with a modest expenditure, we should need or even want a global economy seven
times as large as its present size. Like most other economists, and indeed the general public, Sachs simply assumes
that economic growth is both good and necessary. It apparently never occurs to him to question this assumption, which
Speth demonstrates to be false.

Furthermore, because Sachs maintains that the poorest of
the poor can be put on the path to economic growth with no
more than a very modest redistribution, he seems to assume
that consumption will continue to increase across the board.
He says nothing, however, about what forms of consumption
can continue to multiply without placing yet more pressure
on already overstressed natural systems. Unless the already
affluent are driving even bigger cars, living in bigger houses,
eating higher on the food chain, traveling farther with more
frequency, and buying more electronic gear, what exactly will
they be consuming more of? From what materials will it be
fabricated? What energy sources will be used? In what way

will this increased consumption improve their quality of life? Sachs neither raises nor answers such questions.

Nor does Sachs mention the realities of political power and resource control—for example, the reality that in most instances, poor countries are poor not because they receive too little foreign aid but because we of the rich nations have used our military and economic power to expropriate their resources to consume beyond our own means. It is troubling, although not surprising, that Sachs's reassuring words get an attentive hearing among establishment power holders.

SPETH: REDIRECTION AND REDESIGN

James Gustave Speth, who has degrees in law and economics, has had a distinguished career as the founder and former head of the World Resources Institute, an administrator of the United Nations Development Program, and now dean of the Yale University School of Forestry. Speth writes from the perspective of a systems ecologist.

The End of Growth and Capitalism

In stark contrast to Sachs, Speth concludes in *The Bridge at the Edge of the World: Capitalism, the Environment, and Crossing from Crisis to Sustainability* (2008) that "the planet cannot sustain capitalism as we know it." He recommends that "the operating system of capitalism" be redesigned to support the development of local economies populated with firms that feature worker and community ownership and that corporations be chartered only to serve the public interest.

Rather than settle for a simplistic back-of-the-envelope projection, Speth takes a hard look at the research on GDP growth and environmental damage. He notes that despite a slight decline in the amount of environmental damage per increment of growth, growth in GDP always increases environmental damage. The relationship is inherent in the simple fact that GDP is mostly a measure of growth in consumption, which is the driving cause of environmental decline. Speth is clear that even though choosing "green" products may be a positive step, not buying at all beats buying green almost every time.

> To sum up, we live in a world where economic growth is generally seen as both beneficent and necessary—the more, the better; where past growth has brought us to a perilous state environmentally; where we are poised for unprecedented increments in growth; where this growth is proceeding with wildly wrong market signals, including prices that do not incorporate environmental costs or reflect the needs of future generations; where a failed politics has not meaningfully corrected the market's obliviousness to environmental needs; where economies are routinely deploying technology that was created in an environmentally unaware era; where there is no hidden hand or inherent mechanism adequate to correct the destructive tendencies. So, right now, one can only conclude that growth is the enemy of environment. Economy and environment remain in collision.[5]

After examining the abuses of corporate power, Speth endorses the call to revoke the charters of corporations that grossly violate the public interest, and to exclude or expel unwanted corporations, roll back limited liability, eliminate corporate personhood, bar corporations from making political contributions, and limit corporate lobbying.

Health and Happiness

Speth is clear that we are unlikely as a species to implement the measures required to bring ourselves into balance with the environment so long as economic growth remains an overriding policy priority, consumerism defines our cultural values, and the excesses of corporate behavior are unconstrained by fairly enforced rules. To correct our misplaced priorities, he recommends replacing financial indicators of economic performance, such as GDP, with wholly new measures based on nonfinancial indicators of social and environmental health—the things we should be optimizing. Speth quotes psychologist David Myers, whose essay "What Is the Good Life?" claims that Americans have

> big houses and broken homes, high incomes and low morale, secured rights and diminished civility. We were excelling at making a living but too often failing at making a life. We celebrated our prosperity but yearned for purpose. We cherished our freedoms but longed for connection. In an age of plenty, we were feeling spiritual hunger. These facts of life lead us to a startling conclusion: Our becoming better off materially has not made us better off psychologically.[6]

This is consistent with studies finding that beyond a basic threshold, equity and community are far more important determinants of health and happiness than income or possessions. Indeed, as Speth documents, economic growth tends to be associated with increases in individualism, social fragmentation, inequality, depression, and even impaired physical health.

Social Movements

Speth gives significant attention to social movements that, while grounded in an awakening spiritual consciousness, are creating communities of the future from the bottom up, practicing participatory democracy, and demanding changes in the rules of the game.

Many of our deepest thinkers and many of those most familiar with the scale of the challenges we face have concluded that the transitions required can be achieved only in the context of what I will call the rise of a new consciousness. For some, it is a spiritual awakening—a transformation of the human heart. For others it is a more intellectual process of coming to see the world anew and deeply embracing the emerging ethic of the environment and the old ethic of what it means to love thy neighbor as thyself.[7]

▶◆•◆◀

By this point, given the strength of the evidence to the contrary, it is difficult to take seriously anyone who assumes, without question, that the global economy can expand to seven times its current size by 2050 without collapsing Earth's life support system. Unfortunately, Jeffrey Sachs demonstrates the intellectual myopia common to many professional economists whose ideological assumptions trump reality. When we seek guidance on dealing with the complex issues relating to interactions between human economies and the planetary ecosystems in which they are embedded, we are best advised to turn to those, like James Gustave Speth, who view the world through a larger and less ideologically clouded lens—and who, not incidentally, recognize the distinction between real wealth and phantom wealth.

It is instructive, however, that not even Speth addressed what has become the elephant in the middle of the room—one that had not yet moved to the forefront of the public consciousness at the time he and Sachs were writing their respective books: an out-of-control and out-of-touch financial system devoted to speculation, inflating financial bubbles, stripping corporate assets, and predatory lending. Costly though it has been, the credit collapse has been something of a blessing. It has brought into sharp relief previously obscure but crucial system design choices relating to our financial institutions that we otherwise might not have recognized until they had done so much damage to the economy, our communities, and the environment that recovery would not be possible.

PART II

THE CASE
FOR ELIMINATING
WALL STREET

►•◆•◆•◄

Efforts to fix Wall Street miss an important point. It can't be fixed. It is corrupt beyond repair, and we cannot afford it. Moreover, because the essential functions it does perform are served better in less costly ways, we do not need it.

Wall Street's only business purpose is to enrich its own major players, a bunch of buccaneers and privateers who find it more profitable to expropriate the wealth of others than to find honest jobs producing goods and services beneficial to their communities. They walk away with their fees, commissions, and bonus packages and leave it to others to pick up the costs of federal bailouts, gyrating economic cycles, collapsing environmental systems, broken families, shattered communities, and the export of jobs along with the manufacturing, technology, and research capacities that go with them.

Even more damaging in some ways than the economic costs are the spiritual and psychological costs of a Wall Street culture that celebrates greed, favors the emotionally and morally challenged with outsized compensation packages, and denies the human capacity for cooperation and sharing. Running out of control and delinked from reality, Wall Street has created an Alice in Wonderland phantom-wealth world in which prospective financial claims and the expectations that go with them exceed the value of all the world's real wealth by orders of magnitude.

We can no longer afford to acquiesce to a system of rule by those engaged in the pursuit of phantom wealth far beyond any conceivable need—and to no evident end other than to accumulate points in a contest for the top spots on the Forbes list of richest people.

Chapter 5, "What Wall Street Really Wants," explains why there is no limit to Wall Street greed and how its institutions use the economic and political muscle of their monopoly control of the creation and allocation of money to get what they want: Everything!

Chapter 6, "Buccaneers and Privateers," provides an evocative history of the role that licensed pirates and chartered corporations played in the transition from rule by kings—who found them a cheap substitute for official navies and a useful means of circumventing parliamentary oversight—to rule by global financiers.

Chapter 7, "The High Cost of Phantom Wealth," describes how Wall Street players reap enormous financial rewards for creating phantom expectations through their use of complex financial instruments that defy understanding.

Chapter 8, "The End of Empire," describes Wall Street's rule by the power of money as an extension of five thousand years of imperial rule by kings and emperors who wielded the power of the sword.

CHAPTER 5

▶•◆•◆•◀

WHAT WALL STREET REALLY WANTS

> They honestly believe the source of America's greatness is in its big companies and wealthy elite. And we believe the source of America's greatness is in its middle class and the promise that everybody who works can be rewarded for it.[1]
>
> PRESIDENT BILL CLINTON

The Wall Street money game is a power game, a game as old as empire. And like Monopoly, the popular board game, the game isn't over until the winner has it all. So what does Wall Street want? Everything. And until the crash of 2008, it was on its way to getting it.

The basic question is whether our institutions should be designed to meet the needs of all or to facilitate the Wall Street drive to get it all. Wall Street's answer is clear.

"MODERNIZING" THE ECONOMY

Economist and *New York Times* op-ed columnist Paul Krugman opens *The Conscience of a Liberal* with a personal reflection on growing up in middle-class America with a bipartisan political consensus framed by the New Deal of the Roosevelt administration. As is true for most people of that generation, he grew up believing that a strong middle class supported by a bipartisan political consensus is what America is about.

Only when the New Deal consensus fell apart did he begin to see the deeper truth.

There have been two great arcs in modern American history—an economic arc from high inequality to relative equality and a political arc from extreme polarization to bipartisanship and back again. These two arcs move in parallel: The golden age of economic equality roughly corresponded to the golden age of political bipartisanship.[2]

These arcs, by Krugman's reckoning, are creations of intentional political action. The middle class was created in the space of a very few years by New Deal legislation that created Social Security and other safety net programs, implemented a highly progressive taxation of income and estates, supported unions, and raised the floor on wages—all of which served to

HOW WALL STREET SEES ITSELF

We, the Wall Street money managers, are society's most valuable citizens. We provide capital, manage risk, maintain liquidity in capital markets, and assure the efficient allocation of investment resources needed to create jobs, support innovation, and grow the economy. We are entitled to the fruits of the wealth we create, for as we make our deals, the wealth pie expands, the benefits trickle down, and the lives of all improve.

We fulfill our moral duty to God and country by maximizing individual financial gain, thereby maximizing the gain of all. Those who sacrifice a margin of financial gain for a supposed higher good deprive society of the growth in wealth it might otherwise enjoy, and they thereby engage in an immoral act.

Individualism is the foundation of prosperity and liberty. Government is the enemy of both.

narrow the wealth and income gap between the upper and lower economic classes.

Once in place, this legislative framework was maintained for a time by a new social consensus. Eventually, however, it was reversed by the intentional actions of an alliance of corporate CEOs, religious fundamentalists, antitax libertarians, and neocon militarists. They began mobilizing in the 1970s and launched a political takeover during the 1980s under the banner of the Reagan revolution.

Wall Street corporate interests provided the money and largely controlled the real agenda. The religious fundamentalists provided the votes in return for lip service to a conservative social agenda on abortion, family planning, and gay marriage. The libertarians provided the ideological framework. The neocons provided justification for outsized military expenditures that swelled the profits of the defense industry and secured corporate access to resources and markets. The alliance played up cultural and racial divisions as a diversion, while the moneyed interests pushed through their real agenda, which was to roll back the New Deal and reestablish the elite's power and privilege of the earlier Gilded Age.

Krugman makes a strong case that market forces did not create the middle class and will not restore it. Restoration will come only through political action by a strong political movement.

Certainly, rolling back the policies and gains of the Roosevelt New Deal was a central agenda item for this coalition of right-wing extremists. At least equally important was the effort of its Wall Street wing and their captive regulators —the Federal Reserve and the U.S. Treasury Department—to restructure the U.S. economy in the name of modernization. Their goal was to make finance the economy's dominant and most profitable sector—and they were stunningly successful.

In 1950, arguably the peak of U.S. global power, manufacturing accounted for 29.3 percent of the U.S. gross domestic product and financial services for 10.9 percent. By 2005, manufacturing accounted for only 12 percent of the GDP, and financial services for 20.4 percent. In 2008 financial services was the largest U.S. economic sector, bigger than manufacturing, health, and wholesale/retail.[3] Even more than making our living selling ourselves goods made in China, we have made our living trading pieces of paper—correction: trading numbers encoded in computer files.

Actions to achieve this shift included the removal of restrictions on debt-equity ratios, consumer interest rates, and lending practices, and the formation of huge financial conglomerates that merge banking, insurance, securities, and real estate interests in a densely interconnected web of insider deals. Financial reporting requirements were simultaneously relaxed. These actions cleared the way for the subprime mortgage feeding frenzy that gave us the credit meltdown described in chapter 4.

Hedge funds, the high rollers at the leading edge of the speculative frenzy, proliferated from a couple hundred in the early 1990s to some ten thousand in mid-2007, by which time they had more than $1.8 trillion in financial assets under management. "Like digital buccaneers, and hardly more restrained than their seventeenth-century predecessors," writes political commentator Kevin Phillips, "they arbitraged the nooks and crannies of global finance, capturing even more return on capital than casino operators made from one-armed bandits and favorable gaming-table odds."[4]

BANKING ON SPECULATION

Leveraging—also known as borrowing—became the name of the Wall Street game. Banks used their power to create money to feed the speculative frenzy by creating a complex pyramid of loans to each other. In 2006, by Phillips's calculations, the U.S. financial sector debt, which consists largely of financial institutions lending to other financial institutions to leverage financial speculation, totaled $14 trillion, which was 32 percent of all U.S. debt and 107 percent of the U.S. GDP.[5] According to the Virginia-based Financial Markets Center, in the late 1960s,

> U.S. banks began borrowing Eurodollars in huge volumes from their offshore branches. . . . In each decade since 1969, the ratio of financial sector debt to GDP has nearly doubled. . . . With financial institutions channeling half of new lending to other financial firms, credit markets increasingly are being used less to facilitate economic activity and more to leverage bets on changes in asset prices.[6]

The Wall Street alchemists used a combination of complex derivative instruments, creative accounting tricks, and their capacity to create money from nothing by issuing loans to create phantom financial assets that served as collateral to support additional borrowing to create more phantom assets to. . . . Apparently, some major portion of this trading of loans between financial institutions even involved financial institutions that borrowed from their own branches. Talk about insider trading. Wall Street has no shame.

Gambling with borrowed money is highly risky for both lender and borrower. But the Wall Street players convinced themselves they had eliminated the risk. In their hubris, they seem to have truly believed that they had mastered the art of creating wealth from nothing.

At the time of its collapse, Lehman Brothers was leveraged 35 to 1, which means it financed its gambling in the global financial casino with thirty-five dollars in borrowed money for every dollar of equity. This can be highly profitable in a rising market. It is disastrous when the market is falling and the highly leveraged bets start going bad. Just as gains are leveraged during the rise, so, too, are the losses leveraged during the decline. When others start demanding payment, liabilities can quickly exceed a firm's net equity, which throws the firm into insolvency, as Lehman Brothers and much of the rest of Wall Street learned.

Because they rigged the system to pass the risk to others, the managers who made the losing bets walked away with impressive fees collected during the good times and left to others the messy work of sorting things out when Wall Street's sophisticated version of a Ponzi scheme collapsed. In 2007 alone, the fifty highest-paid private investment fund managers walked away with an average $588 million each in annual compensation—19,000 times as much as an average worker earns. The top five each took home more than $1.5 billion.[7]

In effect, the outsized Wall Street compensation packages represented a looting of the equity that should have been serving as reserves to cover potential losses from the risks inherent in their high-stakes bets. When the bets started going bad, the firms whose equity reserves had been looted went into default. With their bailouts, the Federal Reserve and the Treasury Department—essentially trying to make up for the looted funds—stepped in to cover the losses that should have been covered by the equity that the managers had looted.

That is the Wall Street rule: Capture the gains, pass the risk to others. It appears to be perfectly legal; it should be cause for hard time—and at the least for an effort by government to recover the looted funds on the basis of a dereliction of fiduciary responsibility.

WINNING THE CLASS WAR

Wall Street has been engaged in class warfare pure and simple. It used its control of the money supply and its political influence to ensure that Wall Street players captured virtually all the benefits of productivity gains in the Main Street economy as interest, dividends, and financial service fees. The creation of phantom wealth further diluted Main Street claims to real wealth relative to the claims of Wall Street.

This effort to achieve an upward redistribution of wealth was so successful that from 1980 to 2005, the highest-earning 1 percent of the U.S. population increased its share of taxable income from 9 percent to 19 percent. Most of that gain went to the top tenth of 1 percent and came from the bottom 90 percent.[8]

The measures used to achieve this remarkable outcome included managing monetary policy to maintain a target level of unemployment, managing trade and tax policies to facilitate the corporate outsourcing of jobs to low-wage economies, suppressing labor unions, limiting the enforcement of laws against hiring undocumented immigrant workers, and using accounting tricks that understate inflation to suppress inflation-indexed wage and Social Security increases. As wages fell relative to inflation, and as public services were rolled back, the household savings rate fell apace.

From the beginning of 1959 to the end of 1993, the monthly U.S. household savings rate never fell below 5 percent of household income and often exceeded 10 percent. Since April 2001 it has never exceeded 5 percent, and in the most recent years it has commonly been below 1 percent.[9]

Desperate to find ways to make ends meet, households that experienced shrinking real incomes turned from saving to borrowing. Eager to capitalize on the opportunity thus created, Wall Street used aggressive marketing and deceptive lending practices to encourage people to run up credit card and mortgage debts far beyond their means to repay. As the borrowers inevitably fell behind in their payments, Wall Street hit the victims with special fees and usurious interest rates, creating a modern version of debt bondage. Far from trickling down, wealth rushed upward in a gusher.

As Wall Street exported its modernization plan to the world, the wealth gap widened almost everywhere. The overall scheme was simple. For poor countries, it centered on fielding the World Bank and International Monetary Fund, which encouraged them to fund their development with foreign borrowing. Local elites loved the access to cheap credit and the opportunities to skim off fees and bribes. Foreign contractors got lucrative contracts for large loan-funded projects. And big banks had new customers for loans. It was a win-win all around, except for the poor who got only the bill.[10]

Once the borrowing countries were loaded up with loans far beyond their ability to repay, the World Bank and IMF stepped in as debt collectors and told them:

> Sorry, but since you can't repay, we are here to restructure your economies so we can get back the money you owe us. Eliminate social spending. Cut taxes on the rich to attract foreign investment. Sell your natural resources to foreign corporations. Privatize your public assets and services. Gear your agriculture and manufacturing to production for export to subsidize consumption in rich countries. [Of course, they didn't use the term "subsidize." They probably talked about comparative advantage.] And open your borders to foreign imports. [In theory this was to help domestic manufacturers be more competitive in foreign markets by facilitating duty-free import of inputs.]

Almost every element of the "structural adjustment" worked to the favor of global corporations.

Eventually the Wall Street players realized they could use multilateral trade agreements to circumvent democracy and restructure everyone's economy at the same time. It worked brilliantly.

In 2005, *Forbes* magazine counted 691 billionaires in the world. In 2008, only three years later, it counted 1,250 and estimated their combined wealth at $4.4 trillion. According to a United Nations University study, the richest 2 percent of the world's people now own 51 percent of all the world's assets. The poorest 50 percent own only 1 percent.[11] A 2008 International Labour Organization study reported that in approximately two-thirds of countries studied, income inequality increased between 1990 and 2005. This was in part the result of an overall fall in labor's share of total income relative to that of management and to investment income.[12]

An extreme and growing concentration of privatized wealth and power divides the world between the profligate and the desperate, intensifies competition for Earth's resources, undermines the legitimacy of our institutions, drives an unraveling of the social fabric of mutual trust and caring, and fuels the forces of terrorism, crime, and environmental destruction.

Did the institutions of global finance intend these social and environmental outcomes? Presumably not. The titans of Wall Street are much too focused on competing to be top billionaire to notice the devastated environment or the penniless people at the bottom who have nothing left to be expropriated.

The business press has reported that some hedge fund managers are taking up philanthropy to aid the poor. If any of them have noticed a connection between the power games they plan on Wall Street and the condition of the desperately poor, I've not seen any mention of it.

►·◆·◆·◄

Wall Street presents itself to the public as a financial services sector concerned with and committed to the well-being of people, family, and community. The public-relations image has little foundation in reality. Its real intentions are revealed in what it does, not what it says. Its actions reveal a cultural-institutional complex devoid of morality, which cares for nothing but acquiring money and power by any means.

▶•◆•◆•◀

CHAPTER 6

BUCCANEERS
AND PRIVATEERS

The presidency of Ronald Reagan is commonly referred to as the Reagan "revolution," which sought a restoration of traditional conservative values and free markets. The aggressive deregulation efforts begun under Reagan and carried forward by the Bush and Clinton administrations did indeed restore some traditional conservative values, but perhaps not the ones most U.S. conservatives intended.

Note that the term *conservative* originally referred to the monarchists who fought efforts to establish the democratic accountability of kings. As Wall Street was deregulated, the term regressed to a state reminiscent of an earlier day when the seas were ruled by buccaneers and privateers.

Buccaneer is a colorful name for the pirates of old. The ultimate libertarians, they pursued personal fortune with rules of their own making. They were in their time an iconic expression of "free market" capitalism in its purest form.

Privateers, the forerunners of publicly traded corporations, were pirates to whom a king granted legal immunity in return for a share of the booty.

Wall Street hedge fund managers, day traders, currency traders, and other unlicensed phantom-wealth speculators are the buccaneers of our day, and Wall Street banks are the commissioned privateers. The economy is their ocean. Publicly traded corporations serve as their favored vessels of plunder, phantom wealth is their favored weapon, and the state is their servant-guardian.

Here in brief is the fascinating story of the adventurous forebears of today's Wall Street swashbucklers.[1]

LAUNCHING THE COLONIAL ERA

From the decline of the Roman Empire until 1500, Europe was burdened by the turmoil of endless and pointless wars in which rival noble factions fought one another to exhaustion in a competition to expand their personal power. Imperial rulers enlarged their domains primarily by pushing their borders outward through the military conquest of contiguous territories. The vanquished people and their lands were brought under the central military and administrative control of the city in which the ruling king or emperor resided.

Continuing violence and chaos led to a yearning for monarchs with the power to restore order within stable borders, giving rise to what historians call the modern era. Once the continent was divided into relatively stable domains, Europe's kings satisfied their ambitions for imperial expansion by projecting their power over long sea routes to establish dominion over distant lands, peoples, and resources.

National military forces and colonial administrations remained important to this new model of empire, but for the most part the European kings of the modern era projected their power and augmented their treasuries by granting commissions to favored adventurers, brigands, and corporations who worked for their own account.

Thus began the historic transition from rule by imperial monarchs to rule by imperial corporations, and from the rule of the sword to the rule of money.

ADVENTURERS ON THE HIGH SEAS

Most of us know the period of Europe's drive for colonial expansion primarily by the names of the great adventurers commissioned and financed by their sovereigns to carry out expeditions of discovery, plunder, and slaughter.

In search of a westward sea route to the riches of Asia, Christopher Columbus landed on the island of Hispaniola (present-day Haiti and the Dominican Republic) in the West Indies in 1492 and claimed it for Spain. Hernando de Soto made his initial mark trading slaves in Central America and later allied with Francisco Pizarro to take control of the Inca empire based in Peru in 1532, the same year the Portuguese established their first settlement in Brazil. Soto returned to Spain one of the wealthiest men of his time, although his share in the plunder was only half that of Pizarro. By 1521, Hernán Cortés had claimed the Mexican empire of Montezuma for Spain.

The vast amounts of gold that Spain ultimately extracted from South and Central America ruined the Spanish economy and fueled inflation throughout Europe. With so much gold available to purchase goods produced by others, Spain's productive capacity atrophied as it became dependent on imports. The result was an economic decline from which Spain never recovered.

The pattern is disturbingly similar to that of the current import-dependent U.S. economy—with the primary difference that U.S. imports are financed not by stolen gold but by foreign debt.

Although licensed by the Crown, the celebrated adventurers of old operated with the independence and lack of scruples of crime lords, competing or cooperating with one another as circumstances dictated for personal gain and glory. Their mission was to extract the physical wealth of foreign lands and peoples by whatever means—including the execution of rulers and the slaughter and enslavement of Native inhabitants—and to share a portion of the spoils with their sovereign.

The profits from Spain's conquests in the Americas inspired the imperial exertions of the English, Dutch, and French, who soon divided Africa, Asia, and North America into colonies from which to extract plunder and profits from the monopoly control of trade for the benefit of the mother state.

PRIVATEERS

The competition for foreign spoils among the European powers led to the elevation of the ancient practice of privateering—essentially, legalized piracy—as a major instrument of state policy and a favored investment of both sovereigns and wealthy merchants. Why endure the arduous exertions of expropriating the wealth of foreign lands through conquest and trade when it was much easier to attack and plunder the ships carrying the spoils expropriated by others on their way back to European ports?

Monarchs often found it advantageous to grant a license to privately owned, financed, and captained armed vessels to engage in this profitable enterprise. These privateers offered important advantages to cash-strapped rulers. They provided revenue with no cash outlay, and official responsibility could be disavowed more easily than if the warships of the Crown had pillaged the victim vessels.

Crew, captain, private investors, and the commissioning king divided the revenues from the booty while the king's license lent a patina of legality to the acts of plunder and granted the ships safe harbor. A new era was in gestation from which Wall Street eventually emerged.

Some privateers operated powerful naval forces. In 1671,

Sir Henry Morgan (yes, appreciative kings did grant favored privateers titles of nobility in recognition of their service) launched an assault on Panama City with thirty-six ships and nearly two thousand brigands, defeating a large Spanish force and looting the city as it burned to the ground.[2]

Tax records for 1790 indicate that four of Boston's top five taxpayers that year obtained their income in part from investments in privateering—they included John Hancock, famed for his outsized signature on the Declaration of Independence.[3]

In 1856, the major European powers, with the exception of Spain, signed the Declaration of Paris, declaring privateering illegal. The United States, which relied heavily on privateers as its primary source of naval power and as a major source of commercial profits in its early years, did not stop commissioning privateers until the end of the nineteenth century.[4]

CHARTERED CORPORATIONS

Eventually, the ruling monarchs turned from swashbuckling adventurers and chartered pirates to chartered corporations as their favored instruments of colonial expansion, administration, and pillage. It is instructive to note that in England this transition was motivated in part by the country's incipient step toward democracy.

By the beginning of the seventeenth century, the English parliament, whose establishment was one of the first modern efforts to limit the arbitrary power of the king, had gained the authority to supervise the Crown's collection and expenditure of domestic tax revenues. Chafing under this restriction, sovereigns such as Elizabeth I, James I, and Charles I found that by issuing corporate charters that bestowed monopoly rights and other privileges on favored investors, they could establish an orderly and permanent source of income through fees and taxes that circumvented parliamentary oversight. They also commonly owned personal shares in the companies to which they granted such privileges.[5]

In addition, chartered corporations sometimes assumed direct responsibility for expenses that otherwise would have fallen on the state, including the costs of maintaining embassies, forts, and other naval, military, and trade facilities. English corporations were at times even given legal jurisdiction over Englishmen residing in a given territory.[6]

Corporations chartered by the British Crown established several of the earliest colonial settlements in what later became the United States and populated them with bonded laborers—many involuntarily transported from England—to work their properties. The importation of slaves from Africa followed.

The East India Company (chartered in 1600) was the primary instrument of Britain's colonization of India, a country the company ruled until 1784 much as if it were a private estate.[7]

In the early 1800s, the East India Company established a thriving business exporting tea from China, paying for its purchases with illegal opium. China responded to the resulting social and economic disruption by confiscating the opium warehoused in Canton by the British merchants. This precipitated the Opium War of 1839–42, which Britain won.

The Dutch East India Company (chartered in 1602) established its sovereignty over what is now Indonesia and reduced the local people to poverty by displacing them from their lands to grow spices for sale in Europe. The French East India Company (1664) controlled commerce with French territories in India, East Africa, the East Indies, and other islands and territories of the Indian Ocean.

The new corporate form was a joint stock company, which combined two ideas from the Middle Ages: the sale of shares in public markets and the protection of owners from personal liability for the corporation's obligations. These two features enabled a single firm to amass virtually unlimited financial capital, assured the continuity of the firm beyond the death of its founders, and absolved the owners of personal liability for the firm's losses or misdeeds beyond the amount of their holdings in the company.

Furthermore, separating owners from day-to-day management allowed for a unified central direction that was difficult when management control was divided among a number of owner-partners.

It is no exaggeration to characterize these forebears of contemporary publicly traded limited-liability corporations as, in effect, legally sanctioned and protected crime syndicates with private armies and navies backed by a mandate from their home governments to extort tribute, expropriate land and other wealth, monopolize markets, trade slaves, deal drugs, and profit from financial scams.

►•◆•◆•◄

Publicly traded limited-liability corporations of gigantic scale now operate with substantial immunity from legal liability and accountability even in the countries that issue their charters. They have become the defining institutions of our day. Wall Street is their symbolic seat of power, and they have reversed their relationship to the state.

Wall Street now commissions the state to finance and field the armies that protect its interests and to staff the diplomatic establishment that negotiates treaties in its favor. From time to time, using its ability to crash the economy at will, it extorts protection money in the form of bailouts and Federal Reserve cash infusions. To maintain the state's loyalty, it begrudgingly shares a fraction of its booty in the form of taxes and offers tribute to its politicians as travel perks and campaign contributions.

As did their swashbuckling forebears, Wall Street's buccaneers and privateers seek self-enrichment by plundering
wealth they had no part in creating, enjoy substantial legal
immunity, and acknowledge no duty or accountability other than to themselves. Their success carries a heavy price tag
for the rest of us.

CHAPTER 7

►•◆•◆•◄

THE HIGH COST OF PHANTOM WEALTH

W all Street's relentless drive to have it all not only has had devastating economic, social, and environmental consequences but also has destroyed the integrity of money, created expectations that society has no means to fulfill, and sacrificed the health and happiness of nearly everyone. The full costs are beyond comprehension.

PHANTOM EXPECTATIONS

It is a curious thing that, beyond the money we deposit in an interest-bearing bank account, we expect whatever money we don't immediately spend to grow in perpetuity without much effort on our part. We do not expect real wealth to grow without some serious effort. Buildings must be maintained. Machinery must be replaced. Knowledge must be updated. The trust and caring of a community must be continuously renewed. Skills must practiced. Even wild spaces must be protected from predators, particularly human. All of these require a real investment of time and life energy. Effortless perpetual growth defies the physical law of conservation of energy. Only phantom wealth can grow effortlessly and perpetually.

As our phantom wealth grows, so too do our expectations regarding what constitutes our rightful claim to society's real wealth. Unless we are voluntary simplicity initiates, we are inclined to increase our consumption in tandem with growth in our income, placing an ever greater burden on the planet. So often we say with pride, "I can afford it," without asking whether Earth can afford it.

Because our economic system gives priority to creating phantom wealth, presumed entitlements now far exceed the real wealth available to satisfy them. This can create quite a shock when those of us with financial assets decide to convert our share of the phantom-wealth pool into payments for rent, food, health care, and other needs, if a lot of others make the same decision at the same time.

Financial planner Thornton Parker has pointed out that this is likely to be an issue for baby boomers who built up financial assets during the stock market boom in anticipation of a comfortable retirement. Just as their collective decision to put money into the stock market during their working years helped inflate share prices, so their collective decision to take it out during their retirement will deflate those prices, leaving these retirees in potentially desperate straits.[1]

Wall Street's phantom-wealth machine has created prospective claims and related expectations far out of proportion to the real wealth available to satisfy them.

The problem is not confined to prospective retirees and retirement accounts. It applies as well to the endowments of foundations, universities, and other nonprofits. It applies to the public trust funds of libraries and municipalities, college savings funds, the reserve accounts of insurance companies, personal trust funds, and much else.

There is no way to tell by how much the claims of financial-asset holders exceed the real wealth available to fulfill them, but the evidence suggests the difference is considerable. No one is even asking how the inevitable losses might be fairly distributed. A given dollar doesn't come with a marker that identifies it as a phantom dollar or a real one.

DELINKED FROM REALITY AND
OUT OF CONTROL

The financial figures that get thrown around in relation to the credit crash and financial bailout of 2008 defy both reality and imagination. The financial assets of the richest 1 percent of Americans totaled $16.8 trillion.[2] This represents what they understand to be their rightful claim against the world's real wealth. To put that in perspective, the estimated 2007 U.S. gross domestic product was $13.8 trillion, and the total federal government expenditures that fiscal year were $2.7 trillion.[3]

These sums all seem trifling, however, compared with the $55 trillion in outstanding credit default swaps, which had a central role in the subprime mortgage meltdown. These are essentially insurance contracts that presumably eliminate the risk from the toxic mortgage derivates. They involve bets and counterbets that may partially cancel each other out if anyone can untangle them—but many of the parties to them have already gone bankrupt. Because the transactions were never reported to any central clearinghouse and many of them are carried off the books of the institutions that hold them, no one really knows how much is actually at risk or who owes what to whom.

All we know for sure is that $55 trillion is a great deal of money. It pales into insignificance, however, when compared with the $648 trillion that the Bank for International Settlements reports as the total notional value of all outstanding over-the-counter derivatives as of June 2008.[4] That renders insignificant even the $16 trillion that evaporated between mid-September and the end of November 2008 as the market value of the world's publicly traded corporations' share prices fell by 37 percent.[5]

Is your head spinning? Is your brain shouting, "This doesn't make any sense"? Trust your brain. It is working. Welcome to the Alice in Wonderland world of phantom wealth.

A quick note is in order here on the Wall Street bailout figure of $7.4 trillion noted at the beginning of chapter 1. Perhaps you recall the public outrage in October 2008 when the U.S. Congress passed a bill authorizing the Treasury Department to spend $350 billion to bail out Wall Street financial institutions, with another $350 billion in the pipeline subject to congressional approval. So what is this $7.4 trillion?

Some of it is in established government guarantee and insurance programs, including other Treasury Department programs. The FDIC was on the hook for $1.5 trillion, and the Federal Housing Administration for $0.3 trillion. The bulk of it, $4.5 trillion, was from the Federal Reserve, which acts independently and which routinely makes massive financial commitments to the banking system without any congressional approval or oversight process. Mostly, the Fed creates its own money as it sees fit, with a few simple accounting entries. In most instances, no one seems to know where any particular funding came from, where it was going, or how it was being used.

If you don't understand it, don't feel bad. Nobody seems to fully understand it. The accounting involves so much smoke and mirrors it may be beyond understanding.

What I do know is that over the years I've learned to recognize a system that has delinked from reality and is operating with no one at the helm. Furthermore, I have learned that when folks are moving around trillions of dollars in secret transactions and cannot explain in a credible way where the money is coming from or where it's going, and cannot make a credible case that it is serving a beneficial purpose, they are probably up to no good. In the end, we don't need to know the details to know that Wall Street collapsed because of fatal design flaws in a financial system that needs to be replaced with a system designed to serve the public and to assure accountability.

Now I want to turn to what I believe to be the most important of all the many design flaws of Wall Street's phantom-money machine.

PERPETUAL GROWTH ON A FINITE PLANET

The unrealistic expectation that money should grow perpetually and effortlessly is more than a cultural issue. It is built into the design of the Wall Street money machine. Do you recall the description in chapter 2 of how banks create money with a few computer key strokes when they issue a loan? As I note in chapter 5, they were doing quite a lot of that up until the credit crash. Recall that 32 percent of all outstanding U.S. debt is money that financial institutions owe to each other. By making such loans, banks bulked up their financial statements—and expanded the total amount of money in play in the economy. Recall also that when banks issue loans, they are creating money with simple accounting entries. Yes, much of the phantom-wealth thing is mainly fancy accounting. Perhaps that's why accounting majors are currently the most sought-after business school graduates.

Banks were in fact creating money so fast that the Federal Reserve stopped reporting the most meaningful index of the amount of money in circulation, what economists call M3, on March 23, 2006. Some observers believe the Fed stopped because the amount of money had begun to grow so fast that the M3 might cause alarm and undermine confidence in the dollar.

Phantom Money and Unreported Inflation

John Williams, a consulting economist who has spent years studying the history and nature of economic reporting, tracks economic statistics that the government has either stopped issuing or has seriously distorted. Using the same method-ology the Fed used to use to compile its M3 index, Williams reports that the rate of growth was running from 5 to 7 per-cent in 2005 and began a steady acceleration to a peak annu-al rate of over 17 percent at the beginning of 2008, just before the credit collapse kicked in.[6]

When the money supply expands faster than productive output, price inflation usually results. According to the offi-cial Consumer Price Index, inflation was running at a rate of 2 to 4 percent at the beginning of 2008. Williams compiles his own consumer price index using the same methodology that the government used up until the 1980s, when it decided to start cooking the books to hide evidence of economic mis-management and to keep automatic wage and Social Securi-ty indexing under control. According to Williams the actual rate of inflation at the beginning of 2008 was in the range of 12 to 13 percent. What you experience every time you go shopping is true.

GROWTH AND JOBS

There is a connection between growth and jobs, but only because Wall Street has the system gamed to assure that all the gains from increased productivity go to managers and shareholders rather than to labor.

Thus, total number of jobs will decline and unem-ployment will increase over time if the economy is not growing at a rate at least equal to the increase in pro-ductivity. This problem is easily avoided if productivi-ty gains instead translate into greater time for working people to devote to family, community, and other quality-of-life pursuits.

Surprised? Yes, successive Wall Street–dominated presidential administrations, both Republican and Democratic, have been cooking the books on inflation, and money, and unemployment, and the GDP, for decades. Our economy is in far worse shape than the official statistics reveal. But I stray from our topic.

Inflation of the money supply far in excess of real economic expansion—and the resulting real rate of inflation in consumer prices—is yet another cost of Wall Street's phantom-money orgy. The inflationary phantom money that banks have been creating to fund Wall Street gamblers is one of the several vehicles by which Wall Street takes money out of Main Street pockets and puts it into Wall Street pockets.

Why Debt and the Economy Have to Grow

Because of how our financial system is designed, the economy has to grow or collapse. The growth may or may not provide employment, meet real needs, or reduce poverty. The primary reason that the economy must grow or collapse is the demand of the banking system for its pound of flesh.

Because the bookkeeping entry a bank makes when it issues a loan creates only the principal, the economy must grow fast enough to generate sufficient demand for loans in order to create the money required to make the interest payments. Otherwise debts go into default and the financial system and the economy collapse. The demand for the eventual repayment with interest of nearly every dollar in circulation virtually assures that the economy will fail unless the GDP and income inequality are constantly growing. If you are a Wall Street banker competing for points in the power game, it does not get sweeter than this.

Unfortunately, for the rest of us, this demand for perpetual growth simply to keep the bankers happy results in a serious distortion of priorities. To avoid an economic collapse, policymakers make their choices based not on what will maximize the well-being of all, but on what will generate the greatest financial return to investors to motivate them to take out new loans so enough money will be in circulation to pay the interest due to bankers on the loans already outstanding. The result is ever-increasing debt *and* the accelerating destruction of the natural environment and the human social fabric.

It is illogical and deeply destructive to design an economic system in a way that creates an artificial demand for perpetual growth on a finite planet. Even more pernicious is that the growth must be achieved in ways that continuously improve the financial position of the already rich relative to everyone else.

By contrast, nothing in the design of the formal economic system allows those with little or no access to money even to give voice to their needs, much less fulfill them. They survive only by scratching out their living at the extreme margins of society, in informal or "underground" economies of their own creation. These are design failures of the first order. To heal our sick society, we must redesign our economic system to remove these and other glaring defects, not only to secure our collective survival but also to achieve good health and happiness.

HEALTH, HAPPINESS, AND KEEPING UP WITH THE JONESES

In a society defined by extreme inequality, our perception of our worth and our relationships with others are almost inevitably shaped by our position in the prevailing hierarchy of power and privilege. In this situation we easily fall into the trap of valuing ourselves by our financial net worth and material possessions rather than by our intrinsic self-worth.

Once in the trap, we will likely seek to endear ourselves to those above us even as we scheme to displace them and occupy their more elevated chair. Likewise, we may display contempt, whether overtly or subtly, for those below as a way of affirming our own status. Because financial fortunes are fluid, and great phantom-wealth fortunes can evaporate overnight for reasons wholly beyond our control, we are placed in a position of continuous, sometimes extreme, anxiety, with serious consequences for our physical and emotional health.

In an equitable society in which all people are valued for who they are rather than what they own, our natural concern is for the well-being of the group rather than for our particular position within it. Seeking our place of service becomes more important than defending and improving our position in a power hierarchy. Rather than anxiety, we feel calm exhilaration. Our blood pressure falls and our health and happiness improve.

This is all confirmed by a wealth of scientific studies that document the health and happiness benefits of equality.[7] Stephen Bezruchka, a physician and professor at the University of Washington School of Public Health, sums it up:

> The bigger the income or wealth gap, the more we feel left behind and the harder we work to try to catch up. We feel under pressure to prove ourselves against the measuring stick of self-worth, namely how much we earn and what it can buy us. The invidious comparisons we make with our neighbors (and increasingly with people paraded in front of us by our media) as the models of success, do us in.
>
> Instead of getting what we really want or really need, we want what the rich get! . . . If we are overworking because we are trying to catch up with the Joneses [or maybe Bill Gates], we are very aware of being on a

hierarchical ladder, and that alone, independent of any other factor, worsens our health.[8]

When Ed Diener and his colleagues at the University of Illinois compared the life-satisfaction scores of groups of people of radically different financial means, they found four groups clustered at the top, with almost identical scores on a 7-point scale.

One cluster of respondents, which was composed of people on *Forbes* magazine's list of the richest Americans, had an average score of 5.8. Ah, so money does bring happiness—*at least when you are at the very tip-top of the hierarchy.*

The other three top-scoring clusters were, by contrast, from three groups known for their modest, egalitarian lifestyles and strength of community. These were the Pennsylvania Amish (5.8), who favor horses over cars and tractors; the Inuit of northern Greenland (5.8), an indigenous hunting and fishing people; and the Masai (5.7), a traditional herding people in East Africa who live without electricity or running water in huts fashioned from dried cow dung. These are all communities in which people care for one another and share their resources, and in which economic distinctions are minimal.[9]

By definition, the Forbes 400 list is limited to four hundred people. We cannot all be on it. We could all, however, be living in equitable, caring, sharing communities and enjoying the associated health and happiness benefits. We need only to create societies that put less emphasis on making money and more on cultivating caring place-based communities that distribute wealth equitably.

Wall Street is bad for our health and happiness, not only because it has given us a health care system that places greater priority on Wall Street profits than on our health and well-being, but even more because it destroys a sense of community, creates a narcissistic culture, and rewards predatory competition.

REAL WEALTH WITH NO LIMITS

It is time to stop managing the economy for the benefit of Wall Street bankers and speculators, to ask what we really want from life, and to redesign our economic institutions accordingly. In so doing we should look very closely at evidence demonstrating that once a basic level of material well-being is achieved, the major improvements in our health and happiness come not from more money and consumption, but rather from relationships, cultural expression, and spiritual growth.

These forms of real wealth are most valuable and fulfilling when they are dissociated from money and financial transactions—and they make little or no demand on environmental resources. The title of the classic ballad comes to mind: "The Best Things in Life Are Free." Those words carry a lot of truth. What are the things that give you enduring pleasure? The material needs of people who are secure in their identity and sense of self-worth can be met in quite modest ways, freeing our energy for the things that bring us real joy.

The cover story of the winter 2009 issue of *YES!* magazine is about Dee Williams, a young woman who loves her life in an 84-square-foot house on wheels. It cost her $10,000 to build, including the photovoltaic panels that generate her electricity.[10]

I'll admit that my home office occupies several times the footprint of her entire home. I'd give you odds, however, that she is happier than most of the billionaires that Robert Frank writes about in *Richistan,* who spend their lives rushing between gigantic homes and estates in their private jets and yachts, occupied all the while with making deals by phone and computer to pay the bills.[11]

►•◆•◆•◄

Our economy needs a serious makeover. It is a design issue. We have for too long put up with an economic system designed to make money for rich people and maintain them in a condition of obscene excess, to confine billions to desperation, and to reduce Earth to a toxic waste dump. We can do better. And it's about time we do so. We've put up with this kind of nonsense for five thousand years. Finally, we have the means to choose a different way.

CHAPTER 8

►•◆•◆•◄

THE END OF EMPIRE

L ook still further upstream beyond Wall Street—even beyond
the money-is-wealth illusion—and we find the yet bigger
picture—a five-thousand-year history of rule and expropria-
tion by rulers intent on securing their privilege and pamper-
ing their egos by any means. Call it the era of Empire.[1]

In an earlier time, rulers were kings and emperors. Now
they are corporate CEOs and hedge fund managers. Wall
Street is Empire's most recent stage, and hopefully the last,
in this tragic drama.

Five thousand years is enough. This is an epic moment.
We now have the imperative and the means as a nation and a
species to end the era of Empire and liberate ourselves from a
needless tragedy. Here is the larger story of what is at stake.

THE TURN TO EMPIRE

By the accounts of imperial historians, civilization, history,
and human progress began with the consolidation of dominator power in the first great empires. Much is made of their
glorious accomplishments and heroic battles as imperial civilizations rose and fell.

Rather less is said about the brutalization of the slaves
who built the great monuments, the racism, the suppression
of women, the conversion of free farmers into serfs or land-
less laborers, the carnage of the battles, the hopes and lives
destroyed by wave after wave of invasion, the pillage and

gratuitous devastation of the vanquished, and the lost creative potential.

In the Beginning

According to the cultural historian Riane Eisler, "One of the best-kept historical secrets is that practically all the material and social technologies fundamental to civilization were developed before the imposition of a dominator society."[2] By her account, early humans evolved within a cultural and institutional frame that nurtured a deep sense of connection to one another and to Earth. They chose to cooperate with life rather than to dominate it.

The domestication of plants and animals, food production and storage, building construction, and clothing production were all discoveries and inventions of what Eisler characterizes as the great partnership societies. These societies also developed the institutions of law, government, and religion that were the foundations of complex social organizations. They cultivated the arts of dance, pottery, basket making, textile weaving, leather crafting, metallurgy, ritual drama, architecture, town planning, boat building, highway construction, and oral literature.[3] Indeed, without these accomplishments, the projection and consolidation of imperial power would not have been possible.

The Dynamics of Power

Then, some five thousand years ago, our ancestors in Mesopotamia, the land we now call Iraq, made a tragic turn from partnership to the dominator relationships of Empire. They turned away from a reverence for the generative power of life, represented by female gods or nature spirits, to a reverence for hierarchy and the power of the sword, represented by distant, usually male, gods. The wisdom of the elder and the priestess gave way to the arbitrary rule of powerful, often ruthless, kings. Societies became divided between rulers and ruled, exploiters and exploited.

Mesopotamia, Egypt, and Rome were three of history's most celebrated empires. Each had its moments of greatness, but at an enormous cost in lives, natural wealth, and human possibility, as vain and violent rulers played out the drama of Empire's inexorable play-or-die, rule-or-be-ruled, kill-or-be-killed competition for power. The underlying dynamic favored the ascendance to power of the most ruthless, brutal, and mentally deranged.

Rule by Psychopaths

Social pathology became the norm as the god of death displaced the goddess of life and as the power of the sword triumphed over the power of the chalice. The creative energy of the species was redirected from building the generative power of the whole to advancing the technological instruments of war and the social instruments of domination. Resources were expropriated on a vast scale to maintain the military forces, prisons, palaces, temples, and patronage for retainers and propagandists on which imperial rule depends.

Great civilizations were built and then swept away in successive waves of violence and destruction. Once-great powers, weakened by corruption and an excess of hubris, fell to rival rulers, and the jealous winners sought to erase even the memory of those they vanquished. The sacred became the servant of the profane. Fertile lands were converted to desert by intention or rapacious neglect. Rule by terror fueled resentments that assured repeating cycles of violent retribution. War, trade, and debt served as weapons of the few to expropriate the means of livelihood of the many and reduce them to slavery or serfdom.

The resulting power imbalances fueled the delusional hubris and debaucheries of psychopathic rulers who fancied themselves possessed of divine privilege and otherworldly power. Attention turned from realizing the possibilities of life in this world to securing a privileged place in the afterlife.

Ruling elites maintained cultural control through the institutions of religion, economic control through the institutions of trade and credit, and political control through the institutions of rule making and organized military force. Although elite factions might engage in ruthless competition with one another, they generally aligned in common cause to secure the continuity of the institutions of their collective privilege, often using intermarriage as a mechanism of alliance building.

If many of the patterns associated with ancient kings, pharaohs, and emperors seem strangely familiar to our own time of the democratic ideal, it is because—as elaborated in chapter 6—the dominator cultures and institutions of Empire simply morphed into new forms in the face of the democratic challenge.

A NEW NATION IS BORN

More than two millennia passed between the end of the early democratic experiment of ancient Athens in 338 BCE and the beginning of the West's next democratic experiment, marked by the signing of the Declaration of Independence of the United States of America in 1776.

An Inauspicious Beginning

The realities of life in the English colonies on the Atlantic coast of what was to become the United States of America were not auspicious for democracy. The earliest settlements were operated as privately owned company estates ruled by overseers accountable to British investors. Many of the subsequent settlements were organized as parishes ruled as theocracies by preachers who believed democracy to be contrary to the will of God. The colonial economies depended on slaves and bonded labor, and the family structure placed women in a condition of indentured servitude. The lands the colonies occupied were acquired by the genocidal elimination of Native Americans, and the social structures embodied deep racial and class divisions.

The diversity of circumstances, interests, races, values, religious beliefs, and national origins of the people who made up the new nation speaks to the ambitious nature of the attempt to unite the original thirteen colonies into a great experiment in democracy. Precious little beyond a shared antipathy to British taxes and corporate monopolies bound the people together. They were accustomed to arbitrary rulers at liberty to abuse, or even kill, others with impunity. Most had never experienced any other model of personal liberty. They had no particular reason to consider the law as anything other than a means by which the few exploited the many.

When the People Lead, the Leaders Follow

It is axiomatic that democracy cannot be imposed from above or abroad. True democracy is born only through its practice.

It is a remarkable fact that the American Revolution did not start as an armed rebellion. It originated in a process that looked rather more like a raucous social movement. For all their diversity and lack of experience with organized self-rule, the grassroots rebels who initiated and led the revolution in its earliest manifestations demonstrated a capacity to express the popular will through self-organizing groups and networks—long one of democracy's most meaningful and effective forms of expression.

When the British changed the rules of engagement from nonviolence to violence, the rebels felt compelled to respond in kind.

As the violence escalated, it created a situation that both allowed and compelled the elites of the Continental Congress to assert their authority by raising an army that assumed control of the rebellion and restored imperial order under a new command.

Democracy Betrayed

The other side of history

Once independence was won, the colonial elites who had inserted themselves to take control of what was a self-organized rebellion turned their attention to securing their hold on the institutions of government. The human rights that had been carefully delineated in an earlier Declaration of Colonial Rights, and the principle so elegantly articulated in the Declaration of Independence that all men are created equal and enjoy a natural right to life, liberty, and the pursuit of happiness, fell by the wayside.

The focus shifted to securing the interests of industrialists, bankers, and slave-owning plantation owners and to assuring that the powers of government would remain in the hands of white men of means. Empire morphed once again into a new form, but it remained true to the essential organizing principle of domination. Genocide against Native Americans continued, as did the enslavement of blacks, the denial of the basic rights and humanity of women, and the denial of a just share of profits to those who toiled to make capital productive.

Imperial Plutocracy

What the founders brought forth is best described as a constitutional plutocracy with an agenda of imperial expansion. The British lost to the rebels in the American Revolution, but Empire remained robust in a new nation that ultimately became the greatest imperial power the world has ever known.

The new nation joined together the peoples of thirteen colonies settled on a narrow bit of land along the east coast of North America. This land had been taken by force and deceit from its indigenous inhabitants, and much of it continued to be worked by slaves.

When its leaders decided the lands they occupied were insufficient to their needs, they supported an imperial westward expansion, using military force to expropriate all of the Native and Mexican lands between themselves and the far distant Pacific Ocean.

Global expansion beyond territorial borders followed. The United States converted cooperative dictatorships into client states by giving their ruling classes a choice of aligning themselves with U.S. economic and political interests and sharing in the booty or being eliminated by assassination, foreign-financed internal rebellion, or military invasion. Following World War II, when the classic forms of colonial rule became unacceptable, international debt became a favored instrument for gaining leverage over local economies. Subsequently, economies were forced open to foreign corporate ownership and control through debt restructuring and trade agreements.

THE LONG STRUGGLE

The ideals set forth in the stirring rhetoric of the Declaration of Independence, a revolution, and the U.S. Constitution all failed to bring democracy to North America. They did, however, inspire and lend legitimacy to a long popular struggle of more than two centuries, a global movement that gradually narrowed the yawning gap between reality and ideal in the face of determined and often bloody elite opposition. Within the larger historical context, the accomplishments of the American Revolution, though incomplete, were monumental.

Power of the People

Monarchy became little more than a historical curiosity. In the United States, a clear separation of church and state secures freedom of religious conscience and worship. A system of checks and balances has for over two centuries successfully barred one elite faction from establishing permanent control of the institutions of government. Active genocide against Native Americans ended, and genocide against any group is universally condemned. Slavery is no longer a legally protected institution and is culturally unacceptable.

Native Americans, people of color, people without property, and women have the legal right to vote and to participate fully in the political process. Pervasive though it remains in practice, open discrimination to deny the political rights of any group is culturally unacceptable.

Our taking these accomplishments for granted underscores how far we have come.

A Taste of the Possible

Many of us who grew up in the United States in the post–World War II years came to accept democracy and economic justice as something of a birthright secured by the acts of the founding fathers. We were raised to believe that we were blessed to live in a classless society of opportunity for all who were willing to apply themselves and play by the rules.

The experience of the middle class in those years seemed to confirm this story. Those of us who were a part of it, and I explicitly include myself here, were inclined to dismiss people who spoke of issues of class as malcontents who would rather promote class warfare than accept responsibility for putting in an honest day's work.

Sure, there had been problems in the past, but thanks to America's intellectual genius and high ideals, we had resolved them and rendered them irrelevant to our present. In our arrogance we even believed it our responsibility to make the rest of the world more like us. During my own years of work in Africa, Asia, and Latin America in service to this agenda, I came to realize how wrong we were.

The middle-class ascendance in post–World War II America was an extraordinary demonstration of the possibilities of a democracy grounded in the belief that everyone should share in the benefits of a well-functioning society. Unfortunately, it turned out to be only a temporary victory in the war of the owning class against the rest.

All the disparate popular struggles of our history to achieve justice for workers, women, and people of color, as well as the struggles for peace and the environment, are subtexts of a larger meta-struggle against the cultural mindset and institutions of Empire.

Divided We Fall, United We Stand

The owning classes have long recognized that any political unification of the oppressed places their imperial class privilege at risk. The separate claims of identity politics based on race, gender, and occupational specialization are tolerable to Empire, because they emphasize and perpetuate division. Discussion of class, however, is forbidden, because it exposes common interests and unifying structural issues around which a powerful resistance movement might be built.

Beneath the political stresses that at times threaten to tear our nation apart, we can see the emergent outlines of a largely unrecognized consensus that the world most of us want to bequeath to our children is very different from the world in which we live. Conservatives and liberals share a sense that the dominant culture and institutions of the contemporary world are morally and spiritually bankrupt, unresponsive to human needs and values, and destructive of the strong families and communities we crave and our children desperately need. Deceived by the divide-and-conquer tactics of imperial politics, each places the blame on the other rather than forming a united front to reject Empire's lies and unite to achieve our common dream.

To raise healthy children we must have healthy, family-supportive economies, and that can be achieved only by stripping imperial institutions of their unaccountable power and bringing about an equitable redistribution of real wealth. The struggle for the health and well-being of our children is potentially the unifying political issue of our time and an obvious rallying point for mobilizing a political majority behind a New Economy agenda.

EPIC OPPORTUNITY

It is fortuitous that at the precise moment we face the imperative to do so, we humans have achieved the means to make a collective choice as a species to free ourselves from Empire's seemingly inexorable compete-or-die logic. Three events have created possibilities wholly new to the human experience and have forever changed our perception of ourselves and our possibilities.

1. The United Nations was established in 1945. For the first time in human history it was possible for representatives of the world's nations and people to meet in a neutral space to resolve differences through dialogue rather than force of arms.

2. The first human ventured into space in 1961, allowing us to look back and see ourselves as one people sharing a common destiny on a living spaceship.

3. In the early 1990s, our communications technologies gave us for the first time the capacity to link every

human on the planet into a seamless web of nearly cost-
less communication and cooperation.

Geographical isolation once served well Empire's need to
keep us divided. No more.

The world's estimated 1.5 billion Internet users, 22 percent of all the people in the world, are learning to function
as a dynamic, self-directing social organism that transcends
boundaries of race, class, religion, and nationality to serve
as a collective political conscience of the species.[4] On February 15, 2003, more than 10 million people demonstrated
the power and potential of this technology when they took to
the streets of the world's cities, towns, and villages in a unified call for peace in the face of the buildup to the U.S. invasion of Iraq.

A unified demonstration of political sentiment on this
scale and geographic scope would have been inconceivable
prior to the Internet. This monumental collective action was
accomplished without a central organization, budget, or char-
ismatic leader, through social processes never before possible.
It was not only a demonstration of the transformative power
of our newly acquired technologies, but also an expression of
the awakening of a new human consciousness of our shared
interests and common destiny—and a foretaste of the possibilities for new ways of organizing human affairs.

▶•◆•◆•◀

The source of most of the economic, social, and environmental pathologies of our time—including sexism, racism,
economic injustice, violence, and environmental destruction—originate upstream in institutions that grant unaccountable power and privilege to the few and assign the
majority to lives of hardship and desperation. The history of

the United States demonstrates a simple but profound truth: economic democracy—the equitable distribution of economic power—is an essential foundation of political democracy.

Among the founding fathers of the United States, Thomas Jefferson sought to close the divide between owners and workers by making every worker an owner. Alexander Hamilton sought to secure the position of an elite ruling class by assuring that ownership was firmly concentrated in its hands. Hamilton served as the first secretary of the treasury and laid the foundation of the financial system we now know as Wall Street.

Jefferson had it right, but the Hamiltonians have been winning. Fortunately, the struggle is not over and the financial crash creates a rare opening to rally around the Jefferson ideal of a middle-class economic democracy.

The façade of political democracy has cloaked the extent to which Wall Street financial interests rule our lives and our government. Economic transformation is an essential foundation of the larger political and cultural turning we must now navigate.

It is within our means to create economies that serve rather than exploit. We can have economies that support strong families and communities, afford parents time to give their children loving care, provide high-quality health care and education for all, keep schools and homes commercial free, keep the natural environment healthy and toxin free, and support cooperation and sharing among nations to secure the common good. It is about renewing the democratic experiment, liberating the creative potential of the species, and rediscovering what it means to be fully human.

PART III

AGENDA FOR A
REAL-WEALTH ECONOMY

►◄●◄●◄

Wall Street interests have defined not only the structure of our economy but also the indicators by which we assess its performance. Focused on financial indicators, we accept that the economy is sound even when it is killing us. Real-wealth indicators of the health and well-being of our children, families, communities, and natural systems reveal terminal systemic failure. Since we get what we measure, we should measure what we want.

We humans are awakening to the reality that we are living beings and that life, by its nature, can exist only in community. Our future depends on getting with the program and organizing our economies in ways that mimic healthy living systems—which not incidentally look a lot more like Adam Smith's vision of a market economy than they do Wall Street's.

We have the right, the means, and the imperative to declare our independence of Wall Street and get on with the work of building real-wealth economies that are based on the foundation of what remains of the Main Street economies over which Wall Street presently exercises imperial dominion.

Chapter 9, "What People Really Want," makes the case that the human brain is wired to support caring and sharing and that we humans have long dreamed of a world of vital, healthy children, families, communities, and natural environments: the world we must now create if we are to have a future.

Chapter 10, "Essential Priorities," summarizes the foundational design principles that living real-wealth economies must honor and outlines the opportunities at hand to reallocate real resources in ways that strengthen community, increase equity, bring us into balance with Earth, and increase human health and happiness.

Chapter 11, "Liberating Main Street," sets forth a 12-point agenda for liberating Main Street and banishing Wall Street to the dustbin of history.

Chapter 12, "Real-Wealth Financial Services," spells out a strategy for creating a new financial services sector accountable to the real-wealth needs of Main Street.

Chapter 13, "Life in a Real-Wealth Economy," offers a fictional account of a visit to the future in which our grandchildren may be living if we succeed.

▶•◆•◆•◀

CHAPTER 9

WHAT PEOPLE REALLY WANT

Empire's greatest tragedy is the denial and suppression of the higher-order possibilities of our human nature. The culture and institutions of the Wall Street economy cultivate and reward our capacity for individualistic greed, hubris, deceit, ruthless competition, and material excess. They deny, even punish, our capacities for sharing, honesty, service, compassion, cooperation, and material sufficiency.

The propagandists of Wall Street would have us believe "there is no alternative." They have even given it a name: TINA. To believe them is to give up all hope of a future for our children.

Like most imperial propaganda, TINA is a lie. On the foundation of Main Street, we have the means to build a new economy that cultivates and rewards the best rather than the worst of our nature and thus to realize a long-cherished human dream.

We have allowed Wall Street interests to define not only the structure of our economy but even the indicators by which we assess its performance. So effective is our conditioning to the idea that financial indicators like the GDP are a measure of our progress and well-being that we have for decades been celebrating the "success" of an economy that is killing us.

Here is the real story.

OUR HUMAN NATURE

We humans are complex beings of many possibilities. Empire has demonstrated our capacity for psychopathology. Most people daily demonstrate to one extent or another our capacity for caring, sharing, peacemaking, and service. The former are the possibilities of our lower nature; the latter, the possibilities of our higher nature. Both possibilities are within our means. It is ours to choose which to cultivate.

Cultivating Our Possibilities Rather Than Our Pathologies

The human capacity to choose is perhaps the most distinctive characteristic of our nature. What we are depends in substantial measure on what we choose to be—not just by our individual choices but also by how we shape the collective cultures and institutions that in turn shape our individual behavior.

In previous chapters, we have seen the devastating consequence of cultures and institutions that cultivate and reward our lower nature. We have endured those consequences for five thousand years.

Because cultures and institutions are collective human creations, we can change them through intentional collective action. Given that the cultures and institutions of Empire have survived for five thousand years even in the face of determined popular struggle, we might be forgiven for assuming either that they are immutable or that we are incapable of living any other way. Either conclusion would be wrong.

We have been trapped in Empire's pernicious rule-or-be-ruled, kill-or-be-killed, play-or-die dynamic because of physical and cultural barriers that have kept us divided and unable to see and embrace our common interest. When we were able to breach these barriers and organize in rebellion, we too often saw the goal as being to gain control of the institutions of Empire's power. Those who succeeded in claiming that power with the intention of transforming it all too often became its captive and simply assumed the throne, wearing a cloak of a different color.

The communication technologies of the Internet now in place create a potential for collective dialogue, organizing, and action never before available. We have the means, as well as the need and the right, to bring forth cultures and institutions that cultivate and reward our higher nature. Do we have the will? I believe we do.

The propagandists of Empire tell us that we are by nature a flawed species incapable of caring and cooperation, that we would destroy ourselves but for Empire's controlling, organizing hand. Recent findings from science tell a different and more enabling story: a desire to cooperate and serve is hardwired into the human brain.[1]

Born to Care and Cooperate

Scientists who use advanced imaging technology to study brain function report that the healthy human brain is wired to reward caring, cooperation, and service. Merely thinking about another person experiencing harm triggers the same reaction in our brain as that of a mother who sees distress in her baby's face.

Conversely, the act of cooperation and generosity triggers the brain's pleasure center to release the same hormone that's released when we eat chocolate or engage in good sex. In addition to producing a sense of bliss, it benefits our health by boosting our immune system, reducing our heart rate, and preparing us to approach and soothe. Positive emotions like compassion produce similar benefits.

By contrast, negative emotions suppress our immune system, increase our heart rate, and prepare us to fight or flee.

These findings are consistent with the pleasure that most of us experience being a member of an effective team or extending an uncompensated helping hand to another being.

It is entirely logical. If our brains were not wired for life in community, our species would have expired long ago. We have an instinctual desire to protect the group, including its weakest and most vulnerable members—its children. Behavior contrary to this positive norm is an indicator of serious social and psychological dysfunction. Caring, cooperation, and service are both the healthy norm and wonderful tonics—and they are free.

Traversing the Path from "Me" to "We"

Psychologists who study the developmental pathways of the individual consciousness observe that over a lifetime, those who enjoy the requisite emotional support traverse a pathway from the narcissistic, undifferentiated magical consciousness of the newborn to the fully mature, inclusive, and multidimensional spiritual consciousness of the wise elder. It is a journey from "me" to "we" that over a lifetime traverses from a my-group "we" to a human "we," to a living Earth "we," and ultimately to a cosmic "we."

The lower, more narcissistic, orders of consciousness are perfectly normal for young children, but they become sociopathic in adults and are easily encouraged and manipulated by advertisers and demagogues. The even deeper tragedy is that adults who have been thwarted on the path to maturity are those most likely to engage in the ruthless competition for positions of unaccountable power. Moreover, the Empire system implicitly recognizes that they best embody its values. We have suffered enormous harm from the imperial culture's celebration of the accomplishments of triumphant psychopaths and its promotion of them as the standard of human achievement.

The mature consciousness recognizes that true liberty is not a license to act in disregard of others; rather, it necessarily comes with a responsibility to protect and serve the large we. Doing the right thing comes naturally to the mature consciousness, which minimizes society's need for coercive restraint to prevent the antisocial behavior of those whose path to maturity has been thwarted. This sense of personal responsibility and self-restraint is an essential foundation of a mature democracy, a caring community, and a real-wealth economy. It is one of society's most valuable real-wealth assets.

Strong caring families and communities are not only the key to our happiness and physical health; their emotional support and stimulation facilitate the maturing of our emotional and moral consciousness. They are therefore essential to the realization of our humanity and to the realization of true democracy, a real-wealth economy, and the world of our shared human dream.

THE WORLD OF OUR DREAMS

In 1992, I participated in the civil society portion of the Earth Summit in Rio de Janeiro, Brazil, where I was part of a gathering of some fifteen thousand people representing the vast variety of humanity's races, religions, nationalities, and languages. Our discussions centered on defining the world we would create together.

These discussions were chaotic and often contentious. But at one point it hit me like a bolt of lightning. Despite our differences, we all wanted the same thing: healthy, happy children, families, and communities living in peace and cooperation in healthy natural environments. Out of our conversations emerged an articulation of our shared dream of a world in which people and nature live in dynamic, creative, cooperative, and balanced relationships. The Earth Charter,[2] which is the product of a continuation of this discussion, calls it Earth Community, a community of life.

The Vision We Share

I've lived in a lot of places with starkly different cultures: Ethiopia, Nicaragua, Indonesia, the Philippines, California, Massachusetts, Florida, Virginia, Washington State, and even in a New York City apartment on Union Square between Madison Avenue and Wall Street—which provided an inspiring setting for writing *When Corporations Rule the World*. As I reflect back on this experience, I realize that we humans are a lot more alike than we generally realize. Most of us want to breathe clean air and drink clean water. We want tasty, nutritious food uncontaminated with toxins. We want meaningful work, a living wage, and security in our old age. We want a say in the decisions our government makes. We want world peace.

As Rabbi Michael Lerner, the editor of *Tikkun* magazine, observes:

> The great spiritual-religious wisdom traditions of the world have all taught some variant of this message: The deepest human pleasures come from living in a world based on justice, peace, love, generosity, kindness, and celebration of the universe and service to the ultimate moral law of the universe (whether learned through revelation or through reason).[3]

That should not be surprising. The knowledge is wired into our human brain. The amazing part is the realization that the world we must now create is actually the world that all but the most psychologically deranged human beings want—and that it is within our grasp.

This recognition of our common dream helps answer the question, What is real wealth? The deepest truths seem so obvious once we discover them. Real wealth is a healthy, fulfilling life; healthy, happy children; loving families; and a caring community within a beautiful, healthy natural environment. It is a fulfilling means of livelihood that affirms our inherent worth and service. It is a peaceful world. These are the things of real value and the only truly valid measure of economic performance.

When We Get the Indicators Wrong

We intuitively recognize real wealth when we experience it, but because it is not available for purchase or sale, its value cannot be readily reduced to a monetary equivalent. Economists have dealt with this problem by turning to the market value of economic output as a proxy for human well-being. They call it the gross domestic product. It was a bad choice that has turned our priorities upside down and led to the destruction of much of what is most essential to our health and happiness, including family, community, and nature.

Human health and well-being depend on a great many things that do have market value: food, housing, transportation, education, health care, and many other essentials of a healthy life. These, however, are means, not ends, and their real value is a function of how they contribute to improving human and natural health and vitality.

Note, for example, that the food component of the GDP makes no distinction between healthy and unhealthy food, or between healthy food consumed by a desperately hungry malnourished child and junk food consumed by an overweight compulsive eater. An increase in the market value of food consumed, which increases the GDP, does not necessarily indicate that our well-being has increased.

Or take transportation. An increase in expenditures on transportation, even adjusting for energy-price inflation, may simply mean people are spending more time stalled in traffic jams—hardly an improvement in well-being.

As these simple examples demonstrate, the GDP is a measure of the cost, not the benefit, of economic activity. The GDP can be rising in the face of simultaneous epidemics of child obesity and starvation. It can be rising in the face of dis-integrating families and a vanishing middle class, increasing prison populations, rising unemployment, the disruption of community, collapsing environmental systems, the hollowing out of domestic manufacturing capabilities, failing schools, growing trade deficits, and costly but senseless foreign wars.

You probably noticed that these are not hypothetical examples.

Ever since the end of World War II, we have managed the economy to maximize the economic cost of whatever level of health and happiness—high or low—is actually achieved as an incidental consequence of economic growth. In the face of the economic carnage, politicians point to a rising GDP and tell us with a straight face that the economic fundamentals are sound.

Why in the world would we seek to maximize economic costs rather than the benefits we really want? Perhaps it has something to do with the fact that Wall Street corporations profit from almost all forms of economic activity, whether they're harmful or not; and the Wall Street demand for interest on every dollar in circulation means the economy must grow or crash, as explained in chapter 7. We do it all for Wall Street.

Getting the Indicators Right

You don't need an MBA to recognize that if you manage performance by the wrong indicators, you get the wrong result. We have a desperate need to stop using the GDP as our basis for evaluating economic performance; instead, we must replace it with indicators that show the extent to which the economy is creating and supporting the world we want.

The New Economics Foundation in London has created the most promising index of true economic performance I've yet seen: the Happy Planet Index.† The numerator is a composite of two indicators: life expectancy, which is a simple objective measure of physical health, and life satisfaction or happiness, which is a subjective proxy for mental health. The denominator is the ecological footprint, an indicator of the economy's per capita environmental burden.

$$\text{Happy Planet Index} \quad = \quad \frac{\text{Life Satisfaction} \times \text{Life Expectancy}}{\text{Ecological Footprint}}$$

The result is an indicator of the ecological efficiency with which a society's economy is producing a given level of physical and emotional well-being. The results demonstrate that it is possible to live long, happy lives with a relatively small environmental impact. Generally, island nations and countries with the highest levels of civic participation score the best.

The Pacific island archipelago of Vanuatu scored highest, followed by Colombia, Costa Rica, and the Caribbean island of Dominica. The Western industrial nations generally did poorly. Australia ranked 139, the United States 150, and Russia 172, very near to the African nation of Zimbabwe, which was last at 178.

An aspect of the Happy Planet Index that I particularly appreciate is that it uses only real-wealth indicators. There is none of the distortion inherent in most other financial indicators.

As an ideal, we should assess economic benefits according to nonfinancial indicators reflective of the results we really want. For example, the indicators could measure:

What we want to increase

- the percentage of food grown locally
- attendance at farmers' markets
- school attendance and graduation rates
- voter participation rates
- the number of pedestrian- and bicycle-friendly streets
- the acreage of open space near urban villages
- youth involvement in community service
- the number of neighbors with whom people regularly interact
- the percentage of locally owned businesses
- the size of wild salmon runs

What we want to decrease

- divorce rates
- the number of single parents
- the extent of soil erosion
- incarceration rates
- infant and child mortality rates

- rates of hospitalization for children with asthma
- the total area of impervious surfaces
- childhood obesity rates

Some economists will complain that by using such indicators we would be holding the economy accountable for results that free (unregulated) markets cannot possibly achieve. Take that as an admission that the market must function within a framework of appropriate rules if it is to serve more than the exclusive private interests of the few.

A real-wealth economy is not the sole province of private capital. It is an aggregation of contributions by private capital, government, and civil society, each in proper balance.

NAVIGATING THE TURNING

Think of the work at hand as navigating a great turning from a Wall Street phantom-wealth economy to a Main Street real-wealth economy. In the larger picture, it is a turn from Empire to Earth Community, from an era of domination to an era of partnership.

My wise friend and colleague Puanani Burgess tells the story of a Native Hawaiian navigator who learned and practiced the ancient Polynesian art of navigating to previously unvisited islands thousands of miles beyond the horizon. That ability guided the first Tahitian settlers to Hawaii in the distant past.

Nainoa Thompson made his first solo voyage from Hawaii to Tahiti in 1976 using this ancient practice.

Nainoa Thompson was taught by the master navigator from the Satawal Island in Micronesia, Mau Pialug, to navigate without instruments, using his native wayfinding skills to guide the Hawaiian double-hulled canoe Hokule'a on a Hawai'i-Tahiti voyage of more than 2,200 miles.

As part of Nainoa's training process, Mau would take him to a lookout on O'ahu, where he could see the islands of Moloka'i, Maui and Lana'i. Mau would tell him, "Look beyond the horizon, so that you can see the island you are going to. Especially because you have never been there before, you have to see that island in your mind, or else you can never get there."

That ability—no, courage—to see something you have never seen before is an important part of navigating to the Earth Community that we all long for. Our ability to see it, describe it, share that vision is critical to making it real.

Like the navigators of the Pacific Ocean, the navigators of the Great Turning will require the gifts of mind as well as the heart of someone with the qualities of humility, leadership, courage, and kindness. When we think the journey is hard and impossible, I remember that we made the journey then and now.[5]

▶•◆•◆•◀

Those who join in the work of navigating a great turning from a Wall Street phantom-wealth economy to a Main Street real-wealth economy embark on a bold and courageous journey to a place we have neither been nor seen. We know it only as a deep inner longing. Like the ancient Polynesian navigators, we must look far beyond the visible horizon, form in our mind a vision of the destination we seek, and let that vision be our guide.

▶•◆•◆•◀

CHAPTER 10

ESSENTIAL PRIORITIES

It has been a rude shock for some. After five thousand years of attempting to conquer nature and one another, we humans are waking up to the reality that we inhabit a living spaceship that functions as a community. Our attack on nature is an attack on the life support system on which our every breath depends.

For millennia, our adolescent excesses were little more than an irritant to our Earth Mother, and we got away with behaving as if her patience and abundance were limitless. That time has passed.

We can no longer live by the rules of an open frontier. We must adapt our ways of being and relating to spaceship rules.

We must significantly reduce the aggregate human demand on Earth's natural systems, distribute resources equitably, invest in the regeneration of social and natural capital, and limit—even reverse—population growth through measures that increase equity, strengthen community, and assure access to family planning services. The population-growth dimension is complex and politically controversial, but if we choose not to address it, nature has her own ways of doing it for us through the Malthusian solutions of plague, famine, and intra-species violence.

Wall Street isn't going to be much help here. It excels at increasing aggregate human demand, does even better at increasing inequality, prefers investment in phantom wealth to investment in real wealth, and loves population growth as a source of cheap labor and potential market expansion. Enough said.

Indeed, very little from our economic experience during days on the open frontier is relevant to life on a living spaceship. Humiliating though it may at first seem, we must learn to manage the human economy as a subsystem of Earth's global ecosystem. This will require different indicators, different ways of thinking about and resolving problems, and different ways of relating to one another.

Fortunately, Earth's ecosystems have 3.9 billion years of experience mastering the art and science of spaceship life. We must study and adopt their ways as we accept our adult responsibilities in the larger community of life to which we were born.

ADAPTING TO OUR NEW CIRCUMSTANCES

In his classic essay "The Economics of the Coming Spaceship Earth," economist Kenneth Boulding spells out how life on a spaceship is different from life on an open frontier,[1] where abundant resources are free for the taking, to be used and discarded at will. If such abundance is equally available to all, anyone who complains that another man's fortune is at the expense of his own is properly dismissed as simply too lazy or stupid to take advantage of readily available opportunities. Anyone who applies this same logic on a spaceship is delusional.

From Maximizing Flows to Maximizing Stocks

Boulding notes that a frontier perception that resources are abundant and virtually free has led us to manage our economy to maximize the *flow* of throughput. The GDP, for example, is a measure of the flow of resources through the economy: from resource input, to processing, to consumption, to disposal. To the open-frontier economist, this means that everything else is an externality; that is, it need not be taken into consideration in assessing the costs and benefits of a particular decision. For these economists, externalities include nature, people, and community—pretty much all the things we have identified as real wealth. With such blinkered decision-making rules, the only surprise should be that we are not in even worse shape than we presently are.

Spaceship Rules

In taking the GDP as the measure of economic performance, economists are assuming that the faster resources flow through the economic system to become toxic waste, the wealthier we are. We could get much the same result simply by managing the economy to maximize the rate of growth of our garbage dumps.

Earth's frontier closed sometime during the 1970s, when human consumption of Earth's natural regenerative resources exceeded the limits of what Earth could sustain and many natural systems began to collapse. The collapse began slowly and then accelerated. Our reality has changed; our ways of thinking and doing business have not.

Astronauts hurtling through space in a tightly sealed vehicle understand clearly that their well-being depends on maintaining secure and adequate *stocks* of oxygen, fuel, food, water, and other essentials. Minimizing *flows* and recycling everything is essential to their long-term well-being. Because nothing can be replaced, nothing can be wasted. Consuming faster than stocks regenerate is actively suicidal. Open-frontier cowboys who find themselves suddenly transported to the crew quarters of a spaceship quickly learn new ways or expire.

The frontier is no more. Now it is spaceship rules or death.

No Time for Delay

If you were a fan of the original *Star Trek* TV series, as I was, perhaps you can hear Captain Kirk calling Scotty in engineering. "Kirk to Scotty. Give me a quick status report on life support." "Aye, Captain. It's looking bad." "Scotty, shut down all nonessential systems immediately and transfer all available resources to life support."

Scientists who study such things are now in near universal agreement that to avoid driving Earth's system of climate regulation into irrevocable collapse, we must achieve at least an 80 percent reduction in global greenhouse gas emissions by no later than 2050 and possibly sooner. Given the disproportionate responsibility of the United States for the existing emissions, doing our share will require a reduction closer to 90 percent.

Even if we meet these extremely ambitious goals for reducing greenhouse gas emissions, we face the prospect of significant disruptions of food production due to now unavoidable climate changes, collapsing fisheries, water shortages, and the loss of topsoil. Our problem is compounded by a loss of genetic diversity that reduces possibilities for biological adaptation.

Tempers can flare quickly on a spaceship if a few people consume more than their share and leave others without food, water, and oxygen. The division of Earth's resources is unequal in the extreme, as documented in previous chapters, and the gap continues to grow. Large-scale population displacements from climate-change-induced environmental disruptions are almost certain to increase social tensions and intensify the threat of terrorism and general social breakdown.

Meanwhile, even the most optimistic estimates project a growth in the human population of at least a billion people between now and 2050, while soil erosion, the paving over of farmlands, disruptions caused by climate change, and the depletion of fisheries and freshwater make it a challenge even to maintain current levels of food production.

Neither phantom wealth nor any technology remotely within reach is going to change this grim equation.

ORGANIZING FOR SECURITY AND ABUNDANCE

We might begin by observing how ecosystems organize, and then attempt to mimic what they do. Natural ecosystems have learned to flourish on spaceship Earth. They have much to teach us.

Cooperative Self-Organization

Since the early turn to dominator styles of organization, we humans have been inclined to see life only as a brutal competitive struggle for food, sex, and survival, perhaps to justify our imperial brutality to one another. Life's competitive element makes an important contribution to its dynamism, but competition is only a subtext to the larger story of life's extraordinary capacity for cooperative self-organization.

The secret to life's success is found in the trillions upon trillions of cells, organisms, and communities of organisms engaged in an exquisite dance of continuous exchange with their living neighbors, in which each maintains its own identity and health while contributing to the life of the whole and balancing its own needs against the needs of the larger community. Biologists at the cutting edge of their field now tell us that the species that prosper over the longer term are not the most brutal and competitive, but rather those that find a

PRINCIPLES FOR HEALTHY LIVING SYSTEMS

1. Self-organize into dynamic, inclusive, self-reliant communities of place.

2. Balance individual and community needs and interest.

3. Practice frugality and reciprocity.

4. Reward cooperation.

5. Optimize the sustainable capture and use of energy and matter by adapting to the specific details of the microenvironment.

6. Form and manage permeable boundaries.

7. Cultivate diversity and share knowledge.

niche in which they meet their own needs in ways that simultaneously serve the needs of others and optimize the life of the whole.

In its continuous exchange, life is both frugal and reciprocal. The waste of one species is the food of another in constant and pervasive processes of recycling and reuse.

Because life thrives on diversity and depends on continuous exchange, it exists only in community. An individual organism cannot survive in isolation from other organisms or in a monoculture exclusive to its own species. The greater the diversity of the bio-community and the greater the cooperation among its diverse species, the greater the community's resilience in times of crisis, its potential for creativity in the pursuit of new possibilities, and its capacity to adapt to diverse and changing local conditions.

Self-Reliant Local Adaptation

This capacity for adaptive self-organization allows each of countless local micro-subsystems to adapt to the most intricate features of its distinctive physical microenvironment. Each microsystem is thus able to optimize the capture, sharing, use, and storage of available energy and material resources both for itself and as its contribution to the needs of the larger system. This optimization is possible because an ecosystem is local everywhere it touches Earth.

Local self-reliance in each microsystem's food and energy capture and production maximizes the security and stability in both the local and whole systems. Instead of disrupting the whole system, a disturbance in one part of the system can be more readily absorbed and contained locally. Local self-reliance also creates pressure for each local system to balance its consumption and reproduction with local resource availability, thus serving to maintain balance in the system as a whole.

Managed boundaries are essential to life's existence and its capacity for local adaptation. Living systems have thus learned to form permeable membranes at every level of organization—the cell, the organ, the multicelled organism, and the multispecies ecosystem. At each of these levels, from the individual cell to the ecosystem, the living entity must capture energy from its environment and then maintain it in an active state of continuous flows within itself and with its neighbors. The membrane is also the entity's defense against parasitic predators that would sup on its energies while offering no contribution in return.

If the membrane is breached, the continuously flowing embodied energy that sustains its internal structures mixes with the energy of its environment, and it dies. It also dies, however, if the membrane closes, thus isolating the entity and cutting off the essential energy exchange with its neighbors.

The New Economy as a Living Economy

Because the most important forms of real wealth are living wealth, the term *living economy* is a synonym for a real-wealth economy that mimics the organization of a healthy ecosystem. The measure of a living economy's wealth is the vitality or creative life energy embodied in its people, relationships, and natural environment.

A living economy self-organizes within a framework of market rules. It is rooted locally everywhere, designed to balance its needs for stability with a capacity for creative adaptation to local microenvironments, and structured to be locally self-reliant in meeting most of its energy and other resource needs. Individual enterprises are human-scale and locally owned. Decision-making power is distributed among the community's members in their respective roles as producers, consumers, and citizens.

The culture of a living economy recognizes the mutual responsibility of each individual to balance his or her own needs with his or her responsibility to contribute to the well-being of the whole. Every business enterprise is expected to do the same. Profit is recognized as a means of doing business, not its sole or primary purpose.

As with any living system, the structure of a living economy is defined primarily by its internal flows of energy, which in a human community takes the form of relationships of trust and caring we call *social capital*. Note that I'm not talking here about financial or material flows. I'm talking about flows of life energy, which in a human community means the flows of non-monetized trust and caring essential to community cohesion and vitality. An important asset of a living-economy leader is a flair for organizing participatory street parties.

Recall that permeable managed boundaries are indispensable to life's ability to create and maintain the embodied energy essential to its existence. Each community must have a sense of its own identity and a shared commitment to investing in the human, social, and natural capital crucial to its vitality and capacity to serve its members. To make such investments, it must control its economic resources and priorities.

This does not mean that living economies shut themselves off from the world. To the contrary, they recognize the mutual benefits of fair trade in goods and services and a free exchange of ideas, technology, and culture. But those who come to participate in the local economy are expected to play by local rules and each party to exchanges between neighbors must respect the right of the other parties to determine their own priorities.

In its need to manage its boundary relationships, the Main Street real-wealth, or living, economy comes into a frontal conflict with the interests of Wall Street predators. A living economy depends on local control. Wall Street cries "protectionism" and, in the name of market "freedom" (read: freedom for the market's most powerful players), demands equal access to the community's resources for the exclusive private gain of absentee owners and managers who have neither knowledge of, nor concern for, the community and its priorities.

WALL STREET'S ECONOMIC GLOBALIZATION AGENDA

Wall Street has learned that its ability to generate unearned profits is best served by a system that minimizes local self-reliance and maximizes each locality's dependence on distant resources and markets. A farmers' market where local producers and consumers gather to engage in direct exchanges offers many benefits from a community perspective. The food is fresh, the energy costs of transport are minimal, the personal exchanges grow community, participants can adapt rapidly to changing local preferences and conditions, and the local economy is cushioned from food shocks elsewhere in the world.

Wall Street observes this scene and says: "What's the profit here? We need a global food system in which producers in Chile depend on customers in New York, and vice versa. Then both are dependent on us to serve as middleman. We can set prices on both sides and require producers to buy seeds, fertilizers, and insecticides from us at our prices. The greater our success in convincing foreign producers that they can be more efficient and profitable by specializing in particular products and by trading to meet their needs for a diverse diet, the more they depend on us and the greater our profits."

Wall Street's preference for a system of local monocropping everywhere not only leaves each community dependent on its predatory corporate intermediaries but also decreases global food security.

A weather disruption on one side of the world creates food shortages on the other. If the United States decides to convert its corn crop to ethanol, the price of tortillas in Mexico shoots through the roof. One nation may decide that it is more profitable to pave over its farmland and import food from a place where labor and land are cheaper. It may see the fallacy of such short-term financial calculations only when the supplying country experiences a crop failure and decides to shut off its exports in favor of feeding its own people.

Monoculture cropping is particularly vulnerable to invasive pests or a change in weather conditions. Shipping massive quantities of food around the world breaches natural ecosystem barriers and introduces alien predators against which ecosystems on the receiving end have no defenses.

A community using its own resources to meet its needs is unlikely to have its economy devastated by a business deciding to relocate a major factory. Nor is it likely to suffer a loss of its market because of some sudden shift in the global terms of trade.

Nature is wise and far-sighted. Wall Street is greedy and short-sighted. We do best when we emulate nature.

NEW ECONOMY ALLOCATION PRIORITIES

There is no place on a living spaceship for war, speculation in phantom wealth, advertising to encourage increased consumption, paving over or otherwise destroying or taking productive land out of service, depleting or contaminating water reserves, or engaging in gratuitous displays of material excess. On a spaceship, these are all acts of suicidal insanity and of necessity prohibited. We can and must redirect to more beneficial pursuits the resources that these undesirable activities presently expropriate.

Reclaiming Misallocated Resources

This list of the things that don't work on a spaceship frames a reallocation agenda to meet the most pressing needs of a real-wealth economy. We can reallocate resources from the military to health care and environmental rejuvenation, from automobiles to public transportation, from mining to recycling, from suburban sprawl to compact communities and the reclamation of forest and agricultural lands, from advertising to education, and from financial speculation to local entrepreneurship—to name a just few immediate priorities. This reallocation is the key to reducing the aggregate human burden on Earth while simultaneously improving health and happiness.

The transition will be far from painless, particularly for those employed by institutions of the phantom-wealth economy whose jobs will be eliminated. Wall Street's self-inflicted implosion has helpfully begun the process.

Fortunately for everyone, essential investments in the

New Economy will create far more new green jobs than the number of phantom-wealth jobs that the closeout of the Wall Street economy will destroy. If we do it right, there will be plenty of meaningful work for everyone, including Wall Street refugees and those presently denied a meaningful livelihood—although not with six- to ten-figure compensation packages. For those who find it difficult to adjust to a fair compensation package, I recommend taking a course on the joy and practice of voluntary simplicity.

Military Conversion

Our most certain security threats come from weather chaos, oil dependence, the disruption of food supplies, water scarcity, the social stress of community disintegration and extreme inequality, catastrophic health care costs, and financial collapse. Our primary national security commitment has been to maintain an outsized military establishment, to engage in pointless foreign wars, and to construct new prisons—all of which in the bigger picture make us less secure.

We, the United States, account for roughly half of the world's military expenditures and devote more than half of our federal government's discretionary budget to maintaining our military establishment[2]—to the neglect of education, health, infrastructure, environmental, and other needs. Yet our primary military threats are from a handful of terrorists armed with little more than a willingness to die for their cause.

Students of military science have long known that deploying a conventional military force is futile and counterproductive when fighting unconventional enemies who blend invisibly into the civilian population. The inevitable collateral damage spreads outrage and accelerates the recruitment of terrorists. The only beneficiaries of this stupid security policy are the Wall Street corporations that profit from defense expenditures.

A real security policy would advance a global initiative to renounce war as an instrument of foreign policy, limit our military to a predominantly civilian National Guard home defense force, à la Switzerland, and redirect the human and material resources of the armaments industry to education, health care, environmental rejuvenation, and an energy retrofit of our infrastructure.

Greening Buildings and Rolling Back Sprawl

Low-density urban sprawl consumes prime agricultural and forest lands, reduces food security, increases infrastructure costs, reduces aquifer regeneration, creates auto dependence, undermines community, increases dependence on foreign oil, and increases the toxic pollution of air, land, and water. Rational transportation policies and the reconfiguration of our physical space to bring home, work, school, shopping, and recreation into close proximity can eliminate the need for most private vehicles; recover land needed for agriculture, forests, and natural habitat; and help restore the relationships of community essential to human well-being and happiness.

The construction and maintenance of buildings accounts for a major portion of U.S. energy inefficiency. To meet our target of a 90 percent reduction in greenhouse gas emissions, all new construction will need to meet the *living building standard*, which requires that buildings be at minimum environmentally neutral; preferably, a living building will make a net positive contribution to energy production and to clean air and water. We will also need an ambitious program aimed at retrofitting existing homes and buildings.

It may turn out to be a blessing that much of our national transportation and public infrastructure is in an advanced state of decay due to decades of neglect. The disintegrating system in place is based on an outdated transportation and land-use model. Since we must rebuild, it makes sense to rebuild on a model that promotes energy efficiency, uses renewable energy sources, supports community, and eliminates auto dependence.

Once the transition is complete, the GDP will decline. Security and the quality of life will improve.

Advertising and Public Service Media

The proper role of business in the New Economy is to provide Earth-friendly products and services in response to human needs, not to create artificial wants. Advertising beyond informing the public of the availability and features of products and services has no legitimate place and is not a legitimate business expense. Simply banning advertising would raise complex constitutional free speech issues. There is no constitutional barrier, however, to requiring that the costs of advertising beyond providing basic information on product availability and specifications be paid from after-tax revenues, the same as other forms of speech. Furthermore, there is no legitimate reason to give to Wall Street one of our most valuable public resources—namely, the broadcast spectrum.

The broadcast spectrum is a public commons properly used to serve the public interest. Allowing a few private media corporations to monopolize it to promote narrow private interests while cultivating a culture of individualism, greed, violence, and material excess does not serve the public interest. Independent public and community radio and TV stations representing a diverse range of perspectives should receive substantial preference over absentee Wall Street owners in the allocation of the broadcast spectrum.

►•◆•◆•◄

The transition to an economy suited to the realities of life on a living spaceship poses a significant creative challenge. It also presents an epic opportunity to realize and express our creative potential.

We will need to change virtually every aspect of how we structure and manage our economies. Instead of maximizing the rate at which we turn useful resources into toxic trash, we will need to optimize the health and quantity of our stocks of real wealth, taking care to recycle and reuse in continuous production-consumption loops that convert the wastes of one activity into resources for another. To integrate our lives into Earth's biosystem, we must learn to mimic life's capacity for locally rooted cooperative self-organization. To succeed in these efforts, we must reverse the processes of economic globalization that undermine the efficiency, balance, resilience, and adaptive capacity of real-wealth Main Street economies.

Reallocating resources from harmful or wasteful uses to beneficial ones is a foundational priority of the New Economy agenda. Key items on this agenda include renouncing war as an instrument of foreign policy, dismantling the military establishment, rolling back urban sprawl, and retrofitting our built spaces to restore forest and agricultural lands and wild spaces, strengthen community, increase energy efficiency, and eliminate auto dependence. We will take up other items on the reallocation agenda in following chapters.

Now we turn our attention to the rule changes needed to liberate and renew the Main Street economy so that we humans may thrive on Earth's living spaceship as its sometimes rowdy but hardy and adventurous crew.

CHAPTER 11

>•◆•◆•◄

LIBERATING MAIN STREET

> Proper resentment for injustice attempted, or actual-
> ly committed, is the only motive which, in the eyes of the
> impartial spectator, can justify our hurting or disturbing
> in any respect the happiness of our neighbour. . . . The wis-
> dom of every state or commonwealth endeavours, as well
> as it can, to employ the force of the society to restrain those
> who are subject to its authority, from hurting or disturbing
> the happiness of one another.
>
> ADAM SMITH[1]

W e can and should mourn the trillions of dollars that the Federal Reserve and the U.S. government poured down the drain in an effort to bail out Wall Street. We need not mourn Wall Street itself, however. Bid it adieu, salvage the useful bits for recycling into new forms, and sweep away the rest of the rubble in an economic-renewal campaign to clear the way for building a New Economy on the foundation of Main Street.

Battered by Wall Street, Main Street is struggling for survival, but there are signs that recovery is possible. Even before Wall Street imploded, Main Street was reasserting itself, supported by groups like the Business Alliance for Local Living Economies, the American Independent Business Alliance, the New Rules Project of the Institute for Local Self-Reliance, the Community Food Security Coalition, and other grassroots initiatives across the U.S. and Canada.

These initiatives are demonstrating the potential of human communities for creative self-organization, a potential that has for far too long remained dormant for the lack of a compelling mobilizing vision of possibility. Their efforts are building the foundation of the real-wealth New Economy.

The previous chapter pointed to the depth and possibilities of the change we must now navigate as a nation and as a species. Let me summarize them to be sure we keep them clearly in mind: restructure consumption to achieve a 90 percent reduction in the release of greenhouse gases, achieve an equitable distribution of income, regenerate social and natural capital, eliminate war, and reduce population growth.

Adaptive change of this magnitude requires unleashing the creative potential of the community, which can be done only through responsible self-organization in service to the well-being of the whole. This is the foundational insight underlying Adam Smith's concept of self-organizing market economies.

Market fundamentalists are right in their recognition of the creative potential of self-organization. They are dead wrong in their assumption that this creative potential is optimized by the narrow pursuit of individual financial gain. They miss the essential moral dimension of community life. Self-organization is most effective in optimizing the well-being of all community members when the participants act with a mature moral consciousness of the larger common interests at stake. Moral maturity cannot be mandated, but we can encourage, nurture, and celebrate it, as the local-economy initiatives noted above are doing. We can also establish rules and policies that support positive citizen action and that constrain and punish harmful acts—as recommended by none other than Adam Smith.

NEW RULES FOR A NEW ECONOMY

Government sets and enforces the rules essential to any society whose members do not all measure up to the standard of

ADAM SMITH'S VISION

Adam Smith envisioned a world of local-market economies populated by small entrepreneurs, artisans, and
family farmers with strong community roots, engaged in
producing and exchanging goods and services to meet
the needs of themselves and their neighbors. This was a
vision of the Main Street economy of Smith's time.

Contrary to popular misconception, Adam Smith
was not the father of capitalism. He would have tak-
en offense at the title, because the values of capitalism
as we know it were not his values. He had a substantial
antipathy toward corporate monopolies and those who
use their wealth and power in ways that harm others.
He believed that people have a natural and appropriate
concern for the well-being of others and a duty not to
do others harm. He also believed that government has a
responsibility to restrain those who fail in that duty.

sainthood. These rules combine with the values of a strong
ethical culture to shape the institutions of economic life and
the people and purposes they serve.

The federal government set the rules that created the U.S.
middle class following World War II. When the Wall Street–
led political alliance subsequently took over the government
and changed the rules to favor a wealthier class, the middle
class began to disappear. When it changed the rules again
in order to make finance rather than industry the dominant
economic sector, industrial jobs disappeared, Main Street
struggled for survival, and Wall Street became the largest and
most profitable economic sector.

Citizen action notwithstanding, a turn from a phantom-
wealth economy to a real-wealth economy will require new

rules that favor Main Street and moral responsibility.

Recall the observation in chapter 3 that there is a community-based market alternative to a capitalist economic system run by Wall Street and global corporations. The basic difference between a market system and a capitalist system is rules. A market system has an appropriate set of rules enforced by government to maintain the conditions essential to efficient market function.

Capitalism is what happens in a market without appropriate rules. Economic power becomes increasingly concentrated and turns from the production of real wealth to the production of phantom wealth. A lack of market rules is the cause. The implementation of market rules is the corrective.

Free market ideologues will shout that this is government restricting individual liberty. Liberty can be abused, particularly when combined with a massive concentration of unaccountable financial power, as Wall Street has so dramatically demonstrated. One of government's essential responsibilities, as Adam Smith noted in *The Theory of Moral Sentiments*, is to step in when required to constrain those who abuse their liberty in ways that harm others.

Proper market rules preclude speculation, the acquisition of monopoly power, and the destruction of real wealth to create phantom wealth—all of which are subject to extreme abuse. Proper market rules support an economy that functions more like a healthy ecosystem than a cancer. They create a powerful bias in favor of Main Street and real wealth. They are a good idea.

Wall Street's self-inflicted implosion—and the subsequent exposure of corruption so deep and pervasive that its member institutions ceased lending to one another—have created an opening for serious action. Even the libertarian Alan Greenspan, a dedicated Ayn Rand apostle who as former Federal Reserve chairman had a major role in blocking efforts at regulatory action that might have prevented the Wall Street disaster, has publicly acknowledged that self-regulation doesn't work. The stars have realigned.

Markets absolutely need governments, not to direct every aspect of the economy, but to set the framework of rules within which people and businesses can self-organize in ways that balance individual and community interests.

Some may feel what I am suggesting here goes too far and will ruin the party. Given our situation, my fear is it may not go far enough. The party is over, irrespective of what we do. We have only begun to experience the consequences.

If we act quickly enough to convert to a real-wealth economy, we may avoid living out the future portrayed in some of the darker science fiction accounts of devastated landscapes and roaming gangs.

A 12-POINT NEW ECONOMY AGENDA

I propose a 12-point New Economy agenda. Following are the first 10 points. Points 11 and 12, which are arguably the most important, are addressed in chapter 12, "Real-Wealth Financial Services." They deal with the need to transform financial services and money-supply management to establish accountability to the public interest.[2]

1. Redirect the focus of economic policy from growing phantom wealth to growing real wealth

It's a tried-and-true management maxim: You get what you measure. If the goal is to maximize corporate profits, then assessing economic performance against the growth of gross domestic product may make sense. If the goal, however, is to optimize the health of people and nature, then the use of GDP as a positive measure of economic performance is actively destructive because it leads to policies that promote the growth of phantom wealth at the expense of real social

12-POINT NEW ECONOMY AGENDA

1. Redirect the focus of economic policy from growing phantom wealth to growing real wealth.

2. Recover Wall Street's unearned profits, and assess fees and fines to make Wall Street theft and gambling unprofitable.

3. Implement full-cost market pricing.

4. Reclaim the corporate charter.

5. Restore national economic sovereignty.

6. Rebuild communities with a goal of achieving local self-reliance in meeting basic needs.

7. Implement policies that create a strong bias in favor of human-scale businesses owned by local stakeholders.

8. Facilitate and fund stakeholder buyouts to democratize ownership.

9. Use tax and income policies to favor the equitable distribution of wealth and income.

10. Revise intellectual property rules to facilitate the free sharing of information and technology.

11. Restructure financial services to serve Main Street.

12. Transfer to the federal government the responsibility for issuing money.

and environmental wealth. The use of the stock indices, which tend to be direct indicators of a stock bubble, is even less appropriate.

We must begin a process of replacing financial indicators with indicators of real well-being. Children are society's most vulnerable members. Know the rates of infant mortality, childhood malnutrition, teenage crime, and out-of-wedlock pregnancies, and you have a remarkably clear picture of a society's state of health. For natural systems, biodiversity and the size of fragile fish, bird, and frog populations are excellent indicators of ecosystem health. Imagine how our national economic priorities might shift if we adopted such indicators as our measure of economic performance. You may recall that we discussed nonfinancial indicators at somewhat greater length in chapter 9.

Many economists will dismiss such suggestions with assurances that increasing the GDP is the answer to improving all such indicators. The evidence doesn't bear them out. We need to be shrinking the GDP. Bringing social and environmental indicators to the fore is a start.

Here is the real catch: Shrinking the GDP can be done only in concert with the implementation of agenda item 12, "Transfer to the federal government the responsibility for issuing money." As I explained in chapter 7, private banks create money when they issue a loan, which means that the economy must grow at a sufficient rate to generate new loans to cover the interest due. Otherwise the credit system collapses and the whole economy goes down with it. It is the sword that banks hold over our collective head. "Increase our profits or die." It need not be so, as I will explain in the next chapter. For the moment, just be aware that agenda items 1 and 12 are inseparably linked.

We can in any event raise consciousness of the issues posed by our choice of economic-performance indicators, focus attention on important real-wealth indicators, and get involved in real-wealth indicator projects in our local communities—as people in hundreds of communities in the United States and Canada have already done.[3]

2. Recover Wall Street's unearned profits, and assess fees and fines to make Wall Street theft and gambling unprofitable

We might call this the "close out Wall Street" agenda item. It is not the responsibility of government to save the private institutions of Wall Street that cost us so much and serve us so poorly. Since Wall Street behaves like a criminal syndicate, government should treat it like a criminal syndicate. Prosecute the guilty and require the merely culpable to clean up their act or fold their tents.

I grumble every time I hear business reporters on the evening news refer to stock market results by saying, "Today, investors [did this or that]." Real investors commit funds and their entrepreneurial energy to creating and growing businesses. People who buy and sell pieces of paper in hopes of making unearned gains on price movements are engaging in speculation, otherwise known as gambling, and those who hold the bets and distribute the winnings are bookies. Simply using honest language would help to distinguish between real investors creating real wealth and speculators creating phantom wealth with financial games.

The Wall Street casino has a particular problem in that its players often use other people's money to leverage their bets and can send real-world prices cascading downward—think of the collapsing housing bubble—and create sudden spikes in food and oil prices. Far from stabilizing market prices, as Wall Street touts claim, Wall Street speculation can send prices on wild gyrations.

Let people who want to gamble avail themselves of a licensed casino. Let those who want to invest do so in their

Main Street economy. It's time to recover from the Wall Street bookies what we can of their unearned phantom loot and encourage them to take up honest work by rendering their schemes against society either illegal or unprofitable. Here are a few suggestions.

Legislate an outright prohibition against selling, insuring, or borrowing against an asset you don't really own, and issuing any security not backed by a real asset. With a little investigation, competent regulators can surely come up with a longer list, but you get the idea—and yes, these are all common Wall Street practices that generate substantial quantities of phantom wealth, distort markets, and create instability.

Place strict limits on leveraging by financial institutions and establish reserve and capital requirements for institutions in the business of selling insurance of any kind. Regulate bond-rating agencies and impose strict penalties for fraudulent ratings.

A small financial transactions tax of a penny on every $4 spent on the purchase and sale of financial instruments such as stocks, bonds, foreign currencies, and derivatives would have no consequential impact on real investors making long-term investments in real businesses and assets. But it would discourage much short-term speculation and arbitraging, remove an important source of unearned financial profit, and raise an estimated $100 billion a year in revenue.[4]

Currently, an obscure tax loophole allows hedge fund managers to report their billion-dollar compensation packages as capital gains, which are taxed at only 15 percent. By any measure of justice and good sense, speculators engaged in the creation of phantom wealth should be taxed at confiscatory rates intended to make their games unprofitable. Opponents claim that taxing hedge fund managers will discourage financial innovation. Good. That is exactly the intention.

Assets held for a brief time are usually speculative. Assessing a capital gains surcharge above the normal earned-income tax rate on short-term capital gains would make many forms of speculation unprofitable, stabilize financial markets, and lengthen the investment horizon without penalizing real investors. The capital gains surtax on profit from the sale of an asset held less than an hour should be 100 percent. For assets held less than a week, it might be as high as 80 percent on the otherwise untaxed portion, perhaps falling to 50 percent on assets held more than a week but less than six months.

3. Implement full-cost market pricing

Full-cost pricing is a fundamental market principle. For the market to allocate efficiently, the market price of a good or service must include the full cost of its production and use, including "externalities" like worker, consumer, family, community, and environmental health, which economists and accountants generally ignore. Since Wall Street believes in the power and efficiency of markets, it should be required to play by market rules, which would render it unprofitable.

Eliminating corporate welfare is an obvious starting point. Direct public subsidies to corporations range from resource-depletion allowances to subsidized grazing fees, export subsidies, and tax abatements. Such subsidies should be identified and eliminated.

In 1996, Ralph Estes, a CPA and a professor of accounting, published an inventory of the results of formal studies documenting uncompensated costs that corporations pass on to the public each year—not including direct subsidies and tax breaks such as those just mentioned. The total for the United States came to $2.6 trillion a year in 1994 dollars.[5] This was roughly five times the reported corporate profits in 1994 ($530 billion) and 34 percent of the 1994 U.S. GDP of $6.9 trillion.

Most of the documented externalized costs reflected real-wealth losses, such as worker injuries; the toxic contamination of land, air, and water; and unrecoverable resource depletion. These results reveal a pattern of massive market distortion that put the lie to corporate claims of efficiency and public benefit.

The Government Accountability Office in August 2008 reported that behind the corporate cries of pain over the tax burdens they are forced to bear is a startling truth: Between 1998 and 2005, two-thirds of U.S. corporations paid no U.S. income taxes—zip.[6] Tax loopholes, combined with trillions of dollars of direct subsidies and externalized social and environmental costs, add up to quite a sum.

Actions to recover these costs—by withdrawing official subsidies and tax breaks, assessing fees to compensate for externalized social and environmental costs, and closing tax loopholes and anomalies—will force most of the big corporations either to radically change their business practices or to close shop. Full-cost market pricing will need to be implemented over an extended period to ease the transition. It will likely result in phasing out much of the harmful production that must come to an end anyway, while freeing up resources and market opportunities for Main Street businesses and entrepreneurs.

4. Reclaim the corporate charter

The for-profit private-benefit corporation is an institution granted a legally protected right—some would claim obligation—to pursue a narrow private interest without regard to broader social and environmental consequences. If it were a real person, it would fit the clinical profile of a sociopath. A group of private investors should have the right to aggregate and concentrate virtually unlimited economic power under unified management only if it serves a well-defined public purpose under strict rules of public accountability.

The public purpose of each corporation should be clearly specified in its charter, and the corporation's performance should be subject to periodic review. The charter should be revoked if the corporation consistently violates the law or acts beyond the specific authorities granted. Because political rights belong to people, not to artificial legal entities, corporations should be prohibited from efforts to influence elections or legislation. A first step would be to eliminate all tax exemptions for corporate expenditures related to lobbying, public "education," public charities, or political organizations of any kind. If corporations want to engage in such activities, they should pay with after-tax dollars, as required of real people. You and I don't get tax deductions for our contributions to political lobbyists.

5. Restore national economic sovereignty

It is the right and responsibility of the citizens of every nation to control their own economic resources and to determine their own economic and social priorities, terms of trade, and rules for foreign investors consistent with their needs and values, so long as they internalize the costs of their decisions and do not shift costs onto others. Absentee ownership mediated by global financial markets strips decision making of all but short-term financial values and exclusive private interests.

Communities are best able to set their own economic priorities and achieve economic security when most of their basic needs are met by local businesses that employ local labor and use local resources to meet the needs of local residents for employment, goods, and services. Local owners have a far greater natural interest than absentee owners in managing environmental resources responsibly and sustainably because their own long-term well-being depends on them. Their business decisions are more likely to take into account the health of the community and its natural environment because they will be living with the social and environmental consequences.

The renegotiation of trade agreements should reverse current rules that give global corporations the right to own and operate businesses in any country or community largely free of restrictions and to extract profits at will. New agreements should acknowledge economic sovereignty as a basic community right. Such measures are essential, not only to assure that businesses are accountable to local interests, but also to maintain market vitality and dynamism.

To be mutually beneficial, trade between nations must be in balance. No nation should be living beyond its means on credit offered by another. And no nation should accumulate a long-term claim over the resources of another. The same principle also applies to relationships between communities within nations. It is all part of maintaining system balance.

6. Rebuild communities with a goal of achieving local self-reliance in meeting basic needs

This very sound market principle aligns well with our conclusion in chapter 9: To mimic the processes of stable, productive ecosystems, we must reverse the processes of Wall Street that have led to economic globalization; instead, we must root economic power in communities within a framework of local self-reliance. A policy of local self-reliance creates strong incentives for each community to adapt itself to living within its environmental means—while trading surpluses and freely exchanging information and technology—a much more natural way of life when you are not competing with your neighbors for economic survival.

Economic localization will put an end to the persistent pattern of modern history whereby, through colonization and unbalanced trade and foreign investment, one group lives beyond its means by expropriating the resources of another through force or deceit. It will also bring home a reality that economic globalization largely hides from the eyes of the fortunate: that cataclysmic confrontation looms between consumption and population growth on the one hand and a finite natural resource base on the other.

Achieving local self-reliance will require renegotiating existing trade agreements with the intention of systematically reducing trade dependence; it will also require supporting the efforts of every nation to reclaim its economic sovereignty and to build diversified local economies that use local resources to meet local needs. The goal is a system of fair trade in which localities exchange their surpluses to mutual benefit.

Giving priority to local self-reliance does not mean closing one's borders, but it does mean managing them. Each community must be able to mediate exchanges at its borders with other communities to assure that these are consistent with the integrity and coherence of its internal living processes.

7. Implement policies that create a strong bias in favor of human-scale businesses owned by local stakeholders

Here is another core market principle: Monopoly is a no-no. Wall Street would rather we not notice that the economy internal to a global corporation is centrally planned by corporate managers and directors.

The more an economy is dominated by global corporations, the less it functions by market rules and the more it functions by the quite different rules of oligopoly. Markets are generally more efficient and responsive when served by many smaller firms rather than by one or a few large firms with absentee owners.

Another important benefit of human-scale enterprises is that they encourage relationships of mutual trust and caring. Not only do such organizations tend to be highly productive and innovative, but they also contribute to building and maintaining the social fabric of the community while providing a satisfying work life for their members.

There is less need in human-scale enterprises for hierarchy and bureaucratic control, and a greater possibility for real participation in decision making. Individuals have more scope for exercising creativity and innovation, for developing enduring, caring relationships with fellow workers, and for bringing ethical values into the workplace. All these considerations, from the purely economic to the very human, argue in favor of a strong policy bias in favor of a marketplace served by many small to medium-size enterprises.

Eliminating absentee ownership, broadening ownership participation, and breaking up unaccountable concentrations of corporate power are all foundational elements of a New Economy agenda. A progressive tax on assets—combined with tax breaks for firms owned and managed on a cooperative model by their employees, customers, and those who live in the communities where they are located—can create appropriate incentives to encourage the voluntary breakup of large corporations and their sale to workers or other community investors. Making absentee owners personally liable for harms caused by the corporations in which they hold shares would create another powerful incentive for such restructuring.

Decentralization and deconcentration can be supported by the tightening and rigorous enforcement of antitrust laws to break up concentrations of corporate power. This should be pursued with a presumption that any acquisition or merger, by reducing competition and increasing concentration, is contrary both to market principles and to the public interest.

The burden of proving otherwise should fall squarely on those presenting merger and acquisition proposals.

Much as the decay of our public physical infrastructure creates an opportunity to rebuild on a new model, so too does the decimation of our industrial capacity. We must in a sense reindustrialize, but on a new model of green technology, functional durability, closed-loop product cycles, and zero-emissions production processes.

Where appropriate, smaller firms can join flexible cooperative manufacturing networks of small to medium-size locally owned enterprises, like the famous manufacturing networks of northern Italy. The Mondragón cooperative in Basque Country, Spain, provides another model for strong local-stakeholder ownership. Local retail outlets can form member-owned buying and branding cooperatives like Ace Hardware and True Value.

8. Facilitate and fund stakeholder buyouts to democratize ownership

One of history's most important lessons is that those who own, rule. Even in titular democracies, the powers of ownership readily trump the power of the ballot and play an often decisive role in shaping cultural values. Democracy is strongest when people own the homes in which they live and when they have a direct ownership stake in the assets on which their livelihood depends. When workers are owners, the conflict between workers and owners disappears. When income and ownership are equitably distributed, the market allocates efficiently and responds to the needs of the many rather than the wants of the few.

The federal bailout money that Wall Street corporations are using to buy up smaller rivals would be far better used to support local worker and community buyouts of corporate assets in their communities. Public policy might require a corporation that decides to sell or close a local plant to give the workers or other interests in the affected community an option to buy the assets on preferential terms.

Bankruptcy rules should be structured similarly to give employees and communities the option of taking possession, on preferential terms, of the corporation's remaining assets after bankruptcy proceedings. Similarly, when a company is required to divest parts of its operation under antitrust laws, its employees or the community or both should have the first option to buy the divested units.

Rules governing company pension funds might allow their use by employees to purchase voting control of the firm's assets. Government oversight should structure worker and community buyouts so that workers and communities have real control—in contrast to many employee stock ownership plans (ESOPs) that vest control in management.

9. Use tax and income policies to favor the equitable distribution of wealth and income

As we saw in chapter 8, an equitable society is also likely to enjoy greater health and happiness even at lower overall income levels. Although rarely discussed, equity is an essential requirement of socially efficient market allocation. A strong middle-class society free from the extremes of wealth and poverty is the American ideal.

Market proponents speak enthusiastically about the ability of markets to set priorities based on the real preferences of consumers and to thus achieve a democratic and socially efficient allocation of resources. It would be a valid point—if economic power were equitably distributed. In a world divided between a billion or so people struggling to survive on less than a dollar a day and hedge fund managers each taking in more than a million dollars a day, claims that markets achieve a democratic and socially efficient allocation of resources are more than ludicrous.

Equity doesn't mean everyone has to have the same income. It does mean giving high priority to assuring everyone a means of livelihood adequate to human dignity and to avoiding extremes of wealth and poverty. It means that income policies should assure everyone enough to cover the essentials of a healthful, dignified life and that economic rewards beyond providing for basic essentials should be allocated fairly in proportion to one's contribution to the real wealth of society. By this standard, agricultural workers, janitors, child care workers, elementary school teachers, hospital attendants, and many others would receive more than hedge fund managers, because they all make a greater contribution to the real wealth of society.

Taxes on incomes up to the level required to meet basic needs in a comfortable, satisfying, and responsible way should be eliminated, as should sales or value-added taxes on expenditures for basic food, clothing, shelter, health, personal hygiene, education, and entertainment or recreation. There should, however, be a sharply graduated tax on incomes above the guaranteed minimum—going as high as 90 percent on top income brackets. In addition to a tax of at least 50 percent on estates over a million dollars, inheritance or trust income should be taxed to the receiving individual the same as any other personal income, with appropriate exceptions for family farms and businesses. This would simply restore the progressive tax rates that had a major role in creating the American middle class.

A substantial luxury tax should be levied on nonessential consumption items that are socially harmful or environmentally wasteful or destructive: for example, personal jet aircraft and ocean-going yachts. Personal charitable contributions, including those to family foundations, should be fully tax exempt, thus providing a substantial incentive for individuals with excess incomes to support a strong independent sector as a counterweight to the power of the state and the corporation. Such measures would move us toward more equitable and sustainable societies while maintaining incentives to do socially useful work.

It is perfectly reasonable that those who carry more responsibility be compensated accordingly, but ratios of more than 1,000 to 1 between the CEO and the lowest-paid workers, which is common in U.S. corporations, are unconscionable. Public policy should provide incentives to limit this ratio to no more than 15 to 1. If the top jobs in a corporation or another organization are so difficult or distasteful that qualified applicants can be attracted only with an obscene pay package, then perhaps the corporation needs to be broken up into more manageable pieces.

10. Revise intellectual property rules to facilitate the free sharing of information and technology

Market theory also tells us that for the market to allocate efficiently, buyers and sellers must be fully informed and aspiring entrepreneurs must have free access to relevant technology—no trade secrets. Particularly at this time, when rapid innovation and adaptation are essential to the transition to a new economy, there is an overwhelming public interest in the free sharing of essential information and beneficial technology. Information is the one resource that is nondepletable and increases its real-wealth value when widely shared.

The desire to learn and to innovate is integral to life. Until some twenty to thirty years ago, the driving motivation behind most science was the desire to learn, discover, and share. Academic prestige and rewards came through the publication of new knowledge for others to use, not its monopolization through patents. The idea that needed innovation will be forthcoming only to the extent it is motivated by significant financial rewards is to elevate pathology to a social norm.

The point is not to eliminate intellectual property rights but rather to define them narrowly, grant them for a limited period, and encourage their free sharing.

I take up agenda items 11 and 12, which deal with financial services, in the next chapter.

►•◆•◆•◄

In every instance, what I'm proposing stands the current policy framework on its head. It should not be surprising. The rules presently in place were written by Wall Street lobbyists to favor Wall Street interests. The result is a massive concentration of economic power, the production of phantom wealth, and spreading social and environmental devastation.

The need of our time is to take back the economy, shrink it, and reallocate real wealth to secure the long-term well-being of all. The old rules bar us from doing what we need to do. If democracy has any meaning, we have the right and responsibility to demand that our politicians change the rules that do not serve us—and provide us with financial institutions that do.

CHAPTER 12

>·◆·◆·◁

REAL-WEALTH FINANCIAL
SERVICES

No man can serve two masters: for either he will hate the
one, and love the other; or else he will hold to the one, and
despise the other. Ye cannot serve God and mammon.[1]

JESUS TO HIS DISCIPLES, MATTHEW 6:24

W e've looked way upstream and identified the money
system as the culprit drowning our economic babies
in the river faster than trillion-dollar bailouts and stimulus packages can save them. Pouring more money into Wall
Street is like trying to fill a bucket that has no bottom.

A quick recap.

We have a morally bankrupt money system accountable
only to itself, detached from reality, and driven by unadul-
terated individualistic greed and a misconception of wealth
and money that favors those who create phantom wealth for
those who need and deserve it least at the expense of those
with real needs doing beneficial work. OK. Pause here and
take a deep breath.

We need an ethical money system that is accountable to
the community and is driven by a commitment to serve those
who are creating real wealth, and we need to cut off funding
for swashbuckling privateers engaged in reckless get-rich-
quick speculation that creates economic instability, results
in a misallocation of real resources, and produces nothing of
value in return. Another deep breath.

This is the big picture, and the remedy is clear. The existing system is of the wrong design, and it is corrupt beyond repair. Because it is beyond fixing, we had best devote our attention to replacing it with a new system of a radically different design.

REDUCING DEBT, INTEREST, AND THE PRESSURE TO GROW PHANTOM WEALTH

It seems a bit odd that we have experienced economic collapse because of a credit crunch, an inability to borrow, at a time when the world is awash not only in debt but also in money. *Business Week*'s July 11, 2005, cover story shouted "Too Much Money" and spoke of a savings glut. Its June 11, 2008, European issue reiterated the theme, "Too Much Money, Inflation Goes Global."

Most discussion of the financial crisis focuses on the details and misses the big picture. The problem is twofold. The economic system is awash in money, but it is in the wrong places. Second, virtually every dollar in the system is borrowed, because we rely on banks to create our money by lending it into existence. No debt, no money.

As wages fall relative to inflation, the bottom 90 percent of the population is increasingly dependent on borrowing from the top 10 percent to put food on the table. But when the less fortunate can't repay their loans, the rich people stop lending. Most loans continue to be repaid, but because the default rate is rising and the crazy system of derivatives trading makes it impossible to separate good debts and responsible borrowers from bad debts and deadbeats, banks are afraid to lend to anyone. As the good loans are repaid, the supply of money shrinks because new loans are not being issued.

The demand for real goods and services begins to fall because people don't have the money to pay for them. Businesses lay off workers, who consequently cannot afford either to repay their debts or to put food on the table. The problem appears to be a lack of money, even though the total money in the financial system is far more than enough to cover real-wealth exchanges in a rational real-wealth economy.

It all traces back to a money system that issues money as debt and seeks economic expansion for the sole purpose of generating new demand for debt to create the money to pay the interest on existing debt in an ever-escalating spiral to a never-never land high in the clouds.

A THOUGHT EXPERIMENT

Try this simple thought experiment: Imagine an economy with a stable money supply that neither grows nor shrinks. Money circulates through the economic system steadily and reliably as people engage in their respective trades to produce and exchange goods and services appropriate to their needs.

All jobs pay a living wage, with no more than a modest differential between the highest and lowest paid, and most larger purchases are paid for with savings. Thus, there is no need for consumer credit except for the largest purchases, like a car or home, for which saving enough prior to purchase may not be realistic.

Some people choose to consume less than their incomes would allow. So they put what they save into a term savings account, the equivalent of a certificate of deposit, in a local mutual savings and loan association. In return for agreeing to leave their money in the account for a minimum specified time, they receive a modest interest, say 2 or 3 percent.

The association in turn lends the money deposited by the savers to people in the community who are buying a home or investing in a local business. The association charges 5 or 6 percent on the loan. The interest spread covers its administrative costs and funds a reserve for bad debts. Since it is a mutual association with a cooperative-type membership composed of its savers and borrowers, any surplus at the end of the year may be distributed to the members as a dividend, which means that the money, including the money required to pay future interest, continues to circulate in the community.

Government collects taxes from the community, which it in turn spends in the community to provide for public infrastructure and services as decided through a democratic process. If there is a need to grow or shrink the money supply, the government simply adjusts its taxes and public spending, either to put new money into the economy or to withdraw it.

Everyone participates over time in relatively equal measure as saver and borrower, thus mitigating the tendency for money and real wealth to concentrate in the hands of lenders. Any temporary imbalances are corrected by progressive tax policies. A constant total money supply and the continuous recycling of interest eliminate business cycles and inflationary pressures. Debts are modest and associated with real purchases to meet real needs. In contrast with our current reality, this may sound like some imaginary fairyland, but in fact it is simply a sound design for a real-wealth financial services system.

In this system, government can expand or contract the money supply as needed with a few simple accounting entries to stimulate or contract consumption without the risk of collapsing the money system and thereby the economy. If the community decides that it needs to shrink the economy as part of a larger program to bring its consumption into balance with the natural environment, the government simply reduces its spending relative to its tax receipts and extinguishes a portion of tax receipts by reversing the accounting entries by which it created that money in the first place.

This is a very simplified model of how the money system of a real-wealth economy might function, but it is helpful in visualizing where we want to go. Apart from the structural issues, the model assumes both a popular awareness of the difference between phantom wealth and real wealth, and a commitment to radical equity and community well-being. It also assumes away Wall Street. Since it doesn't assume away money or the need for financial institutions, getting where we want to go requires replacing Wall Street with a new real-wealth system of money and finance.

FINANCIAL SERVICES AGENDA

Now we can turn to the last two items on the 12-point New Economy agenda outlined in the previous chapter: restructuring financial services to serve Main Street, and transferring to the federal government the responsibility for issuing money. As with the presentation of the first 10 agenda items, my intention here is to provide a direction and a framework for policy action, not a blueprint.

11. Restructure financial services to serve Main Street

It wasn't long ago that independent, locally owned banks devoted to meeting the financial needs of their local Main Street economies were the foundation of the U.S. banking system. They served community needs rather like the banks in the thought experiment above.

Then, as rules against bank mergers were relaxed, local banks consolidated into regional banks that were acquired by Wall Street banks. The whole banking system turned from serving Main Street to serving Wall Street, and from creating real wealth to creating phantom wealth. To restore the real-wealth economy we need to reverse this process.

The Wall Street collapse creates the opportunity. We need only turn the Wall Street bailout into a salvage operation aimed at claiming and recycling its useful bits.

Ellen Brown, the author of *The Web of Debt*, points out

that the government has a number of options for dealing with a failed bank, one of which is to buy shares of its stock and assume ownership.[2] In the early stages of the 2008 Wall Street bailout, the Treasury Department under Secretary Henry Paulson bought shares of troubled banks but promised not to interfere with management.

More than interfere, the Treasury Department should take control of failed banks, oust the management, and begin a radical restructuring and divestment process by selling their retail units to local investors to operate as independent community banks. Alternatively, they might be spun off as member-owned mutual savings and loan associations managed on a cooperative model.

Either way the newly liberated banks would operate under strict federal and local oversight as regulated utilities in the classic textbook banking role of financial intermediary between local people looking to secure a modest interest return and other local people who need a loan to buy a home or finance a business. Mergers between banks would be prohibited as they once were under our unitary banking laws.

12. Transfer to the federal government the responsibility for issuing money

Bank lending at interest isn't the only way to create money. Critics of our present money-debt system have long called for a system of nondebt government issuance. A government institution would create needed money the same way that private banks now do, with an accounting entry. Instead of lending it into existence, however, government would spend it into existence to meet a public need, preferably a public investment in infrastructure, education, or technology development.[3]

The common objection to such proposals is that giving politicians the power to create free money would lead to abuse and runaway inflation. This argument is a bit disingenuous given the Wall Street record of enthusiastically fueling the inflation of tech-stock shares in the 1990s and home prices in the current decade. Its record on consumer price inflation isn't much better. Critics have documented the intentional falsification of the consumer price index to understate the real rate of inflation we experience in our day-to-day shopping experience. When calculated using the methods in place in the 1980s, they report that the real rate of inflation of consumer prices is ranging between 12 and 14 percent.[4]

The risk that government will abuse its money-creation powers can be minimized through a combination of separation of powers and public transparency. An independent federal agency would decide how much new money to create. The Congress would decide how it would be spent. And by law, the whole process would be transparent and open to public scrutiny.

It wouldn't be perfect, but it would be far less subject to abuse than the present system, under which the Federal Reserve functions as an arm of Wall Street to decide how much money to create and who gets it, creating and allocating trillions of dollars to favored private Wall Street institutions without public disclosure or oversight.

Under a properly designed system of government issuance, the money would serve public purposes and reduce the need to collect taxes. Since the money is spent rather than lent, it need not be repaid, and it circulates permanently, thus eliminating the boom-and-bust cycles almost inevitable in the current system. If government decides to reduce the money supply, it simply cancels a portion of the money received in taxes through a reverse accounting entry.

As I come to understand the power of accounting, I marvel that I once thought it was a boring subject. I don't recall anyone in business school mentioning that it is accountants who really rule the world.

Obviously, a proposal to transfer the power to create money from bankers to government would elicit deafening screams and prophecies of imminent doom from Wall Street. Fortunately, the Wall Street implosion has reduced to rock bottom its credibility and the public sympathy for its tender sensibilities.

HOW WOULD WE DEAL WITH . . . ?

You may find yourself asking, Without Wall Street how will we deal with consumer credit, retirement, and insurance? Each presents a need for which we tend to look to financial institutions for solutions—and each does have its financial dimension. As always, however, we need to look upstream for the bigger picture, because each has an essential nonfinancial dimension as well. The transition to the New Economy must address both.

Consumer Credit

There is limited place in the New Economy for consumer credit. It has assumed such importance in our current economy largely because Wall Street turned credit cards into a substitute for paying a decent wage. A real-wealth economy that pays families a living wage is a pay-as-you-go economy that discourages borrowing to cover current expenses. Borrowing to purchase larger durables like homes and autos is a different matter, and these needs are best met by borrowing from a neighborhood community bank or savings and loan.

To maintain the convenience of paying with plastic as a substitute for writing checks, New Economy community banks and savings and loan associations can form a transaction-clearing system owned cooperatively by its member institutions, much like Visa once famously was.

Retirement

Do you remember the Malaysian forestry minister back in chapter 2 who wanted to cut down all the trees and put the money in the bank to earn interest? Debates about individual retirement accounts and putting Social Security money in a lockbox are based on the same phantom-wealth fallacy.

Retirees cannot eat money. They need real food, shelter, medical care, clothing, recreation, and other goods and services—all of which must be produced and provided by working people at the time the needs are presented.

In the real world, retirement is necessarily a contract between retirees and the working people who agree to devote a portion of the fruits of their labor to providing for the retirees' needs. The threat facing future retirees is not insufficient money; it's demographics.

In 1935, when the newly signed Social Security bill set the retirement age at 65, males at birth had a life expectancy of 60 years. Life expectancy rose to 74 by 2005 and is expected to grow to 85 years by the end of this century. But the accepted retirement age has stayed the same, creating an increasingly impossible burden on the working population to provide ever-longer extended vacations for those who reach 65.

In 1960, there were five working people per retiree. Because of longer life spans and the greater percentage of people reaching retirement age, that ratio was 3.3 to 1 in 2004 and, unless the retirement age changes, will be down to 2 to 1 by 2040.[5] At some point working people struggling to keep their children fed and clothed will say, "Enough already."

The basic design of Social Security is sound, but there is no financial solution to the threat to Social Security's continued viability. We must change the retirement age as part of a larger real-wealth restructuring of the economy and the workforce.

The answer to a secure retirement will not be found in the financial services sector. It will be found in a recognition that we all need to remain active contributors to the real-wealth economy for as long as we are able, and that we need to rely on a universal Social Security system to manage the intergenerational transfer of real wealth to care for our needs once active engagement is no longer practical.

Insurance

Insurance, which is essential to our health and security, involves joining a group that agrees to share risks that are predictable for the group, but can be neither avoided nor predicted for the individual. Rather than self-insuring, which most people simply don't have the financial means to do, we need to pool our risks, which Social Security and Medicare do extremely well insofar as they can go.

Insurance does not lend itself to a pure private-profit maximization approach. The temptation is simply too great to identify and exclude the high-risk individuals who most need help and to pocket the premiums and skimp on the reserves required to pay claims. If the choice is for a private, for-profit insurance system, it must be highly regulated.

A far more workable and efficient approach is a single-payer federal program, similar to Social Security and Medicare. A third, more decentralized option is a system of member-owned mutual insurance societies as were common before Wall Street changed the rules and converted them to Wall Street–owned for-profit corporations.

Even with a single-payer approach or mutual-insurance society, however, there is a limit to how far we can go in dealing with risks as purely a matter of pooling the costs.

Previously insurable risks are escalating out of control, as we see with medical care costs and losses from natural disasters like hurricanes and wildfires. Again, we must look upstream and take steps to deal with the causes of the risk.

Take health insurance. Our focus is on the cost of health services. If we look upstream, however, we see the toxic contamination of our air, water, soil, and even the food we eat. We see an excessive consumption of junk food prepared with too much salt and sugar. We see sedentary lifestyles. Rather than providing more funding for health insurance, we need to deal with these upstream causes. We can take actions to increase the availability of nutritious food to inner-city residents, ban junk food from schools, lower the overall sugar and salt levels in processed foods, provide easy access to home and neighborhood primary health care à la Cuba, and lay out public spaces in ways that encourage walking and bicycling. And don't forget the big one, the physical and mental health benefits of equity we discussed in chapter 7.

We need a similar approach to reducing the impact of catastrophic weather events, which are almost certain to increase. We must deal with the cause by reducing carbon emissions while at the same time investing in remediation actions such as improving levees, removing brush, changing land-use patterns, and revising building codes.

Above all we must keep in mind that our best insurance when tragedy does strike is a strong and resilient community that mobilizes quickly for mutual assistance.

▶◆◆◆◀

We have given the proponents of unrestrained greed more than twenty-five years to show us what their immoral philosophy can do for us. The results are definitive. It is time for a new approach based on mutual responsibility and accountability, the essential foundations of a real-wealth New Economy.

Obviously, the underlying structures, beliefs, and values of an economy designed to turn over control of society and its resources to buccaneers and privateers with a passion for phantom wealth are very different from those of an economy designed to root economic power in equitable middle-class communities of place committed to environmental steward-ship. The 12-point agenda for a New Economy can serve as a navigation chart.

Before turning to part IV on implementing strategy, let's make a brief visit to the future to see how our children might be living in 2084 if we regain our sanity as a species and suc-ceed in navigating the turning from a phantom-wealth econ-omy to a real-wealth economy.

CHAPTER 13

>•◆•◆•◄

LIFE IN A REAL-WEALTH
ECONOMY

The idea of deep and potentially wrenching change can be frightening. I have written this fictional account of life in the real-wealth New Economy in the hope it may make such a life easier to visualize. I trust you will recognize the application of the principles outlined in previous chapters.

Some may be inclined to dismiss this hopeful vision as nothing more than a naïve flight of fancy far beyond any possibility of becoming a reality. Anyone who has followed my writing knows I have a clear understanding of what a serious fix our species is in and what the barriers to change are.

I sometimes suffer fits of despair and wonder whether there is any reason not to just give up, turn off the news, and live out my remaining days in quiet solitude. I suspect anyone who doesn't experience similar feelings from time to time is seriously out of touch with reality.

That said, I know from experience that the story I sketch below is consistent with an almost universally shared human dream and with the core values of both conservatives and liberals. The most common exceptions are people who have retreated into terminal cynicism born of deep despair and who no longer dare to hope that another way might be possible. But to give in to despair is to create a self-fulfilling prophecy.

That so many people share a dream consistent with the world we must now create is my primary source of hope that we may succeed in mobilizing the will to make the collective choices outlined in these pages.

Imagine a time machine has projected you into a future in which the real-wealth New Economy prevails. You find yourself in a world of culturally vital, high-density middle-class communities nestled together in the midst of lush farmlands and natural habitats. Here is your report to the folks back home.

Dear friends and fellow bloggers back in 2009:

My trip to the future has been an experience far beyond my expectations. I landed in 2084 in the United States, in a place very near where I grew up. I had been rather nervous about the whole thing, given the financial, social, and environmental disasters I left behind. It is pretty amazing to know how it worked out.

The history books tell of difficult times as the disasters you are experiencing played out, but people in communities all over the world rallied to the cause and created a new economy from the bottom up. The politicians eventually realized what was happening and jumped on the bandwagon just as it was about to pass them by. I love the result and would be tempted to stay and settle here permanently if that were an option, but the terms of my travel don't permit it—and I do miss you all.

Let me share a bit of what I'm seeing and experiencing. I think it will give you a sense of hope and strengthen your commitment to the New Economy agenda we were discussing before I left. Much of what I'm seeing validates the ideas we talked about. Feel free to share this report with others in the hope it may inspire them as well. So here goes.

This seems to be a truly middle-class society. I've found little evidence of more than modest distinctions between the richest and the poorest in terms of income, asset ownership, size of residence, and consumption. Most families own their own homes and have an ownership stake in one or more businesses in their local economy. Paid employment seems to be organized to allow everyone ample time for family, friends, participation in community and political life, healthful physical activity, learning, and spiritual growth. People seem to be using that time fully.

Economists in this time measure wealth and well-being by indicators of the health and sustainable productivity of human, social, and living natural capital. Businesses are human-scale, locally owned, and dedicated to serving the people of the community. They take great pride in their contribution to securing the well-being of their community's children for generations to come.

I've seen no evidence of the grotesque, monotonous suburban sprawl so familiar to our own time. An old-timer told me that in the old days, as the price of oil became prohibitive, people began to abandon the suburbs. Rising energy costs and climate chaos disrupted long-distance food supply chains, and building materials became scarce. Governments responded by spending billions to deconstruct abandoned suburban buildings, salvage the materials for reuse in constructing new dwellings in compact communities, and then removed the asphalt and rebuilt the soils to support organic farming, grazing, and timber production.

Agrochemicals were banned. People seem to compost or recycle just about everything. I asked about waste dumps, but no one seemed to understand what I meant. They just don't throw things away.

I've learned that publicly traded for-profit global corporations went the way of the suburbs. Those that produced useful products were broken up into their component businesses and sold to their employees or to the communities in which they were located. Others eventually went bankrupt. Their intellectual assets were released to the public domain, and useful physical assets were sold at public auction.

The overall quantity of consumption appears to be modest by our standards, but the health and vitality of the children and of family and community life seem far richer. In my travels around the region, I'm impressed by the diversity of wildlife, the healthy appearance of forests and waterways, and the evident fertility of the soil.

Living off financial returns from passive investments, financial speculation, collecting rents, gambling, and other unproductive activities is so unfamiliar that people are incredulous when I try to explain it to them. Their question is always the same: "Why would a civilized society tolerate anything like that?"

I get a similar puzzled response when I ask about crime and war. They say crime is rare. Some recall reading about war, terrorism, the arms industry, and outsized military budgets in history books, but they apparently have no experience of such things.

People here live in compact communities in modest but comfortable energy-efficient multifamily dwellings that run primarily on wind and solar power. Most live within walking or bicycling distance of their jobs and the local stores that supply their daily needs. Motor vehicles are relatively rare with the exception of a few buses, taxis, and essential commercial vehicles. Travel of any distance is by public transit, primarily rail. International travel is rare and generally by rail or by wind- or solar-powered ship.

Far from a sense of isolation, however, there is a deep sense of membership in a global village. Everyone these days is

connected to everyone else by a global electronic communications network that supports virtually free personal
exchanges, videoconferencing, and the sharing of live cultural performances. You all know how excited I was about
being able to use my laptop to talk for free on Skype vid-
eo with my wife back home when I was visiting Australia in
2008.

Well, let me tell you, that seems so primitive given what
is possible here. Holographic imaging capabilities have
become so advanced I find myself forgetting I'm not actually sitting across the table from the people I'm talking with. I
do miss the hugs.

The database capabilities are equally amazing. Everyone has
free instant access to pretty much the total body of human
experience, information, knowledge, and technology. The
speed of innovation is remarkable now that everyone has
a basic education and is able to so easily share the lessons
of their local experiences in strengthening community and
enhancing the health and productivity of their local biosys-
tems. I must admit I experience a serious sense of information overload, but the young people seem to handle it with
remarkable ease.

In my conversations with people about their way of life, I've
been impressed by the pride and joy people take in contributing to the care of their local streams and forests and participating in community life. Everywhere I go there seems
to be some sort of neighborhood party, potluck, or cultural event. It reminds me of when I visited the island of Bali
in Indonesia back in 1961. Everyone I meet seems to have
a meaningful and dignified vocation that contributes to the
well-being of the larger community and fulfills his or her
basic needs for healthful food, clean water, clothing, shelter,
transport, education, entertainment, and health care.

As I dig deeper, I find that intellectual life and scientific inquiry are vibrant, open, and dedicated to the development and sharing of knowledge and life-serving technologies that address the society's priority needs. It is amazing how motivated people are to express their creativity when given the opportunity.

I'm also struck by the evident strength and stability of the families I've met. Children are all well nourished, receive a high-quality education, and live in secure and loving homes. It seems that nearly everyone is involved in civic and political life. Suicide, divorce, abortion, and teenage pregnancy are so rare that when they do occur, they are news events and spark lively discussions among people curious to learn what went wrong and how it might be avoided in the future.

I guess this also explains why crime is nearly nonexistent. Those who have difficulty following the rules become the focus of a community rehabilitation program. There are a few prisons for those who seem to be beyond redemption, but prisons are considered a sign of social failure, and the goal is to eliminate them entirely.

Perhaps my biggest shock was finding that people here respect their politicians for their wisdom, integrity, and commitment to the public good. I'm told that in this time people go into politics out of a sincere desire to serve, and they find that the political system encourages and rewards integrity. Maybe that's because after pouring trillions into a Wall Street bailout following the credit collapse of 2008, we eventually shut down Wall Street and brought an end to its perverse influence over our culture and politics.

With much love and hugs to you all.

▶•◆•◆•◀

My greatest source of sadness comes from an awareness of the profound gap between our human reality and our human possibility. My greatest source of joy comes from my awareness of the vitality of the human spirit as expressed by the millions and millions of people who are working to realize their shared vision of a just and sustainable world that works for all. My greatest source of motivation is my belief that it is within our collective means to make that vision a reality and that we each have a responsibility to do everything within our means to actualize that possibility.

PART IV

CHANGE THE STORY, CHANGE THE FUTURE

▶•◆•◆•◀

Barack Obama was swept into the U.S. presidency on a promise of change. Like those who came before him, however, he has no doubt learned that those who hold the world's most powerful office are captive to its imperatives.

In President Obama's case, the imperatives include appeasing Wall Street interests that are part of his political base. Not only did Wall Streeters provide substantial funding for his campaign and for many members of the House and Senate, they also have the power to bring the economy to a standstill if his policies displease them. To act against Wall Street, the president must be confronted with a popular demand from below too powerful to be ignored.

There is an instructive parallel between our present situation and that of the early American settlers who mobilized to declare their independence from the rule of a distant king. Then as now, leadership in dismantling the institutions of Empire did not come from within the institutions of Empire; it came from a powerful social movement that mobilized from below. Deep transformational change is unlikely to be achieved in any other way.

The power of popular movements resides in their ability through dialogue to change the stories that frame the collective life of the society and through their actions to create new cultural and institutional realities. People throughout the United States and the world are already engaged in this work of birthing the New Economy (by whatever name they might call it).

Chapter 14, "An Address I Hope President Obama Will One Day Deliver to the Nation," presents my high dream for a future presidential announcement of a national policy commitment to a real-wealth New Economy agenda.

Chapter 15, "When The People Lead, the Leaders Will Follow," draws out the parallels between the self-organizing resistance movements of the earlier colonists who achieved their independence from British rule and the subject colonists of our day who through their actions are declaring their independence from Wall Street rule. It concludes by outlining a strategy for citizen action.

►·◆·◆·◄

CHAPTER 14

AN ADDRESS I HOPE PRESIDENT OBAMA WILL ONE DAY DELIVER TO THE NATION

B arack Obama was elected to the U.S. presidency on a promise of change. Before his inauguration, indeed before his election, I drafted the following as my dream for the economic address he might deliver to the nation during his administration in fulfillment of the economic aspect of that promise. It is the New Economy agenda presented in the style of candidate Obama's political rhetoric.

I suffer no illusion that he will deliver it. He has surrounded himself with advisers aligned with Wall Street interests in an effort to establish public confidence in his ability to restore order in the economy. Because there has been no discussion of any other option, to most people "restoring order" means restoring the status quo with the addition of a job-stimulus package, and that is most likely what he will try to do.

This speech presents the missing option—the program that a U.S. president must one day be able to announce and implement if there is to be any hope for our economic, social, and environmental future. It is up to those of us committed to making the New Economy a reality to prepare the way by popularizing the vision in the public mind through public dialogue, the subject to which I turn in chapter 15.

Here is the address.[1]

Fellow Citizens:

My administration came to office with a mandate for bold action at a time when our most powerful economic institutions had clearly failed us. They crippled our economy; burdened our federal, state, and local governments with debilitating debts; divided us between the profligate and the desperate; corrupted our political institutions; and threatened the destruction of the natural environment on which our very lives depend.

The failure can be traced directly to an elitist economic ideology that says if government favors the financial interests of the rich to the disregard of all else, everyone will benefit and the nation will prosper. A thirty-year experiment with trickle-down economics that favored the interests of Wall Street speculators over the hardworking people and businesses of Main Street has proved it doesn't work.

We now live with the devastating consequences: a disappearing American middle class and a crumbling physical infrastructure; failing schools; millions without health care; dependence on imported manufactured goods, food, and energy, and even essential military hardware. At the same time it has increased our burden on Earth's living systems and created an often violent competition among the world's peoples and nations for Earth's remaining resources.

Wall Street became so corrupted that its major players no longer trusted one another. The result was a credit freeze that starved legitimate Main Street businesses of the money they needed to pay their workers and suppliers. Pouring still more taxpayer money into corrupted institutions didn't, and won't, fix the fundamental problem.

Corrective action begins with recognition that our economic crisis is, at its core, a moral crisis. Our economic institutions and rules, even the indicators by which we measure economic performance, consistently place financial values ahead of life values. They are brilliantly effective at making money for rich people. We have tried our experiment in unrestrained greed and individualism. Our children, families, communities, and the natural systems of Earth have paid an intolerable price.

We have no more time or resources to devote to fixing a system based on false values and a discredited ideology. We must now come together to create the institutions of a new economy based on a values-based pragmatism that recognizes a simple truth: If the world is to work for any of us, it must work for all of us.

We have been measuring economic performance against GDP, or gross domestic product, which essentially measures the rate at which money and resources are flowing through the economy. Let us henceforth measure economic performance by the indicators of what we really want: the health and well-being of our children, families, communities, and the natural environment.

I call on faith, education, and other civic organizations to launch a national conversation to identify the indicators of human and natural health against which we might properly assess our economic performance, taking into account what we know about the essential importance of equity, caring communities, and the vitality, diversity, and resilience of nature to our overall physical and mental health and well-being.

The GDP is actually a measure of the cost of producing a given level of human and natural health and well-being. Any business that sought to maximize its costs, which is in effect how we have managed our economy, would soon go bankrupt—and indeed it has brought our nation to the edge of financial, as well as moral, bankruptcy. We will henceforth strive to grow the things we really want, while seeking to reduce the cost in money and natural resources.

No government on its own can resolve the problems facing our nation, but together we can and will resolve them. I call on every American to join with me in rebuilding our nation by acting to strengthen our families and our communities; to restore our natural environment; to secure the future of our children; and to reestablish our leadership position and reputation in the community of nations.

Like a healthy ecosystem, a healthy twenty-first-century economy must have strong local roots and maximize the beneficial capture, storage, sharing, and use of local energy, water, and mineral resources. That is what we must seek to achieve, community by community, all across this nation, by unleashing the creative energies of our people and our local governments, businesses, and civic organizations.

Previous administrations favored Wall Street, but the policies of this administration henceforth will favor the people and businesses of Main Street—people who are working to rebuild our local communities, restore the middle class, and bring our natural environment back to health. Together we can actualize the founding ideals of our nation as we restore the health of our nation and its economy.

- We will strive for local and national food independence by rebuilding our local food systems based on family farms and environmentally friendly farming methods that rebuild the soil, maximize yields per acre, minimize the use of toxic chemicals, and create opportunities for the many young people who are returning to the land.

- We will strive for local and national energy independence by supporting local entrepreneurs who are creating and growing local businesses to retrofit our buildings and develop and apply renewable-energy technologies.

- It is a basic principle of market theory that trade relations between nations should be balanced. So-called free trade agreements based on the misguided ideology of market fundamentalism have hollowed out our national industrial capacity, mortgaged our future to foreign creditors, and created global financial instability. We will take steps to assure that our future trade relations are balanced and fair as we engage in the difficult but essential work of learning to live within our own means.

- We will rebuild our national infrastructure around a model of walkable, bicycle-friendly communities with efficient public transportation to conserve energy, nurture the relationships of community, and recover our farm and forest lands.

- A strong middle-class society is an American ideal. Our past embodiment of that ideal made us the envy of the world. We will act to restore that ideal by rebalancing the distribution of wealth. Necessary and appropriate steps will be taken to assure access by every person to quality health care, education, and other essential services, and to restore progressive taxation, as well as progressive wage and benefit rules, to protect working people. These policies are familiar to older Americans because they are the policies that created the middle class, the policies with which many Americans grew up. They were abandoned by ideological extremists to the detriment of all. We will restore them, with appropriate adaptation to current circumstances.

- We will seek to create a true ownership society in which all people have the opportunity to own their own homes and to have an ownership stake in the enterprise on which their livelihood depends. Our economic policies will favor responsible local ownership of local enterprises by people who have a stake in the health of their local communities and economies. The possibilities include locally owned family businesses, cooperatives, and the many other forms of community- or worker-owned enterprises.

My administration will act at the national level to support your efforts to advance these objectives at the local level by engaging in a fundamental reordering of our national priorities.

Because the world can no longer afford war, the foreign policy of this administration will be crafted to build cooperation among people and nations in order to eliminate terrorism and its underlying causes; resolve conflicts through peaceful diplomacy; roll back military spending and demilitarize the economies of all nations; restore environmental health; and increase economic stability.

We will work to replace a global system of economic competition with a global system of economic cooperation based on the sharing of beneficial technology and the right of the peoples of each nation to own and control their own economic resources to meet their needs for food, energy, shelter, education, health care, and other basic needs. We will work to protect the rights and health of working people and the environment everywhere.

An unprecedented concentration of power in transnational corporations that owe no allegiance to any nation, place, or purpose undermines democracy, distorts economic priorities, and contributes to a socially destructive concentration of wealth. Corporate charters give a group of private investors a special legal right to aggregate and concentrate economic power under unified management. The only reason for a government to grant such a charter is to enable a corporation to serve a well-defined public purpose under strict rules of public accountability. I am appointing a commission to recommend legislation that redefines the corporate charter so that each corporation's designated public purpose is specified in its charter and periodically subject to public review.

There will be no more government bailouts of failed corporations during my administration. Any private corporation that is too big to fail is too big to exist. We will institute vigorous antitrust enforcement to break up excessive concentrations of economic power and to restore market discipline.

Because absentee ownership invites irresponsibility, we will create incentives for publicly traded corporations to break themselves up into their component units and to convert to responsible ownership by their workers, customers, or small investors in the communities in which they are located.

Through a public legal process, we will withdraw the charter from, and force the dissolution of, any corporation that consistently fails to obey the law and fulfill a legitimate public purpose.

There is no place in a life-serving twenty-first-century economy for financial speculation, predatory lending, or institutions that exist primarily to engage in these illegitimate practices.

We will act to render Wall Street's casino-like operations unprofitable. We will impose a transactions tax, require responsible capital ratios, and impose a surcharge on short-term capital gains. We will make it illegal for people and corporations to sell or insure assets that they do not own or in which they do not have a direct material interest. The brain power and computing capacity now devoted to trading electronic documents in speculative financial markets will be put to work solving real social and environmental problems and financing life-serving Main Street enterprises that create living-wage green jobs.

To meet the financial needs of the new twenty-first-century Main Street economy, we will reverse the process of mergers and acquisitions that created the current concentration of banking power. We will restore the previous system of federally regulated community banks that are locally owned and managed and that fulfill the classic textbook banking function of serving as financial intermediaries between local people looking to secure a modest interest return on their savings and local people who need a loan to buy a home or finance a business.

And last, but not least, we will implement an orderly process of monetary reform. Most people believe that our government creates money. That is a fiction. Private banks create virtually all the money in circulation when they issue a loan at interest. The money is created by making a simple accounting entry with a few computer keystrokes. That is all money really is, an accounting entry.

Many years ago our government gave private banks the exclusive power to create money through the issuance of debt. This means that someone has borrowed and is paying interest to a private bank for virtually every dollar in circulation. The more our economy expands, the greater the debt owed to the bankers who create the money essential to economic exchange.

This makes banking a very profitable business, but it creates inherent economic instability as credit expands and contracts. Furthermore, because banks create only the principal loaned, but not the interest, the debt-money system creates an imperative for perpetual economic expansion to generate new loans to create new money at a sufficient rate to allow borrowers to pay the interest due on their loans. This means the economy must grow to keep the money supply from collapsing and assures that as a nation we are mired in ever-growing debt.

U.S. household mortgage and credit card debt stood at $13.8 trillion in 2007, roughly the equivalent of the total 2007 GDP, and much of it was subject to usurious interest rates. The federal debt inherited from the previous administration stood at $5.1 trillion in 2007, before the Wall Street bailout was approved, and it cost taxpayers $406 billion a year in interest alone, the third-largest item in the federal budget after defense and income transfers like Social Security.

This debt hamstrings our government and places an intolerable burden on American families that undermines physical and mental health and family stability. It also creates a massive ongoing transfer of wealth from the substantial majority of households that are net borrowers to the tiny minority of households that are net lenders. This engenders a form of class warfare that has become a serious threat to the security of America's working families.

There is another serious consequence of giving control of our money supply to Wall Street. When Wall Street banks stop making the accounting entries needed to fund Main Street, the real-wealth economy collapses, even though we have willing workers with needed skills and still need to meet the needs of our families, maintain the nation's physical infrastructure, and protect our natural resources. The economy stops solely because no one is making the necessary accounting entries to allow real businesses to function. We cannot allow the moral corruption of Wall Street to bring down our entire economy, indeed our entire nation.

My administration will act immediately to begin an orderly transition from our present system of bank-issued debt money to a system by which money is issued by the federal government. We will use the government-issued money to fund economic-stimulus projects that build the physical and social infrastructure of a twenty-first-century economy, being careful to remain consistent with our commitment to contain inflation.

To this end I have instructed the treasury secretary to take immediate action to assume control of the Federal Reserve and begin a process of monetizing the federal debt. He will have a mandate to stabilize the money supply, contain housing and stock market bubbles, discourage speculation, and assure the availability of credit on fair and affordable terms to eligible Main Street borrowers.

By recommitting ourselves to the founding ideals of this great nation, focusing on our possibilities, and liberating ourselves from failed ideas and institutions, together we can create a stronger, better nation. We can secure a fulfilling life for every person and honor the premise of the Declaration of Independence that every individual is endowed with an unalienable right to life, liberty, and the pursuit of happiness.

▶•◆•◆•◀

There is an inevitable and necessary division of duties in the work at hand. President Obama assumed office inheriting a failed economy, pervasive economic desperation, a bankrupt treasury, wars in Iraq and Afghanistan, a federal bureaucracy weakened by the willful appointment of incompetent ideologues, climate change, peak oil, and a crumbling national infrastructure. His essential priority will be to clean up the monumental mess left by the previous administration.

President Obama has little choice but to work within the economic and governmental institutions that bear major responsibility for creating the mess in the first place. He immediately demonstrated his commitment to recruiting the most competent and experienced people he could find to help him, which inevitably meant people with long years of experience serving these institutions.

Those of us who work in and through Main Street businesses and civil society organizations had best think of our situation as akin to that of the early American colonists who declared their independence from a distant British monarch and his rapacious chartered corporations. They declared their liberty by refusing to accept the authority of the king's appointees and acted to create a new reality more to their liking.

The political leaders now known as the founding fathers eventually signed a Declaration of Independence and raised an army. They acted, however, only after the people had mobilized and a self-organized popular rebellion was well established.

Wall Street is our monarch. The Obama administration is our equivalent of the founding fathers.

In the case of the American colonists, once the people led, the leaders followed. That is our metaphor, and creating a new reality of liberty from Wall Street is our cause.

►•◆•◆•◄

CHAPTER 15

WHEN THE PEOPLE LEAD, THE LEADERS WILL FOLLOW

Whoever tells the stories of a nation need not care who
makes its laws.

ATTRIBUTED TO ANDREW FLETCHER, SCOTTISH
PATRIOT (1653–1716)

It is time to stop trying to fix what can't and shouldn't be
fixed, declare our independence from Wall Street, and get
on with building the New Economy and a new system of
financial institutions designed to serve it. There are inter-
esting parallels between our situation and that of the early American colonists who decided the time had come to
declare their independence from a distant king. Wall Street
is a formidable foe, but so was Britain, which at that time was
the most powerful empire on Earth. Fortunately, the ultimate
advantage lies with a motivated and organized citizenry.

We don't know whether or when the Obama administration will join us in a people's declaration of independence
from Wall Street and its phantom-wealth machine, as the
founding fathers eventually joined the people in their rebellion against British rule. The one thing of which I am certain, however, is that for it to happen, we the people must
first show the way.

HOW BIG CHANGE HAPPENS

One of the advantages of reaching one's elder years is having lived through enough history to experience how rapidly deep change can happen—and how committed groups can shape and accelerate it.

Change the Story

I have witnessed the great social movements of our time, including the civil rights, women's, and environmental movements. Each began with a conversation among a small group of people that rapidly expanded and ultimately challenged a false cultural story that justified the particular oppression the movement sought to end. As the story changed, so too did history. It was accomplished through conversations that built a social consensus around a new story, and through actions that created a new reality and gave concrete expression to the benefits of a different way of doing things.

For the civil rights and women's movements, the old story said: *Women and people of color have no soul. Less than human, they have no natural rights. They can find fulfillment only through faithful service to their white male masters.* For the environmental movement, the old story said: *Nature was given to man by God to do with whatever man pleases. It has no value beyond its market price.*

To change the course of history, we must discredit the cultural stories on which the old ways rest and replace them with new cultural stories that point to a new course.

A Global Declaration of Independence from Wall Street and Its Global Counterparts

Chapters 6 and 8 placed the Wall Street colonization of the U.S. economy in the historical context of a larger human

WITNESSING HISTORY

My belief that an economic restructuring of the magnitude I am proposing is possible reflects my personal experience with the transformative power of social movements.

In my early youth, I rode a bus in Miami in which "colored" people were confined to the last rows. It was beyond imagination that I would live to witness whites weeping tears of joy over the landslide election of a black president.

Fran, my wife, was warned by her father when she went off to college that if her grades were too high, no man would marry her. She had a straight-A average when I met her. I married her anyway—a smart choice, as it turned out—but assumed without question that she would follow me without complaint and subordinate her career to mine. Years later, she was the primary wage earner and I happily and productively followed her, fashioning my career to fit hers.

In 1994, when I was writing *When Corporations Rule the World*, corporations were acting with impunity to circumvent democracy and consolidate their power, using trade agreements to rewrite the rules of global commerce. There was little public awareness that trade agreements were an issue. In 1999, a historic Seattle protest brought the powerful World Trade Organization to its knees in a shock from which it never recovered.

struggle against five thousand years of Empire. The civil rights, women's, and environmental movements are all expressions of this larger struggle.

So too is the global resistance against Wall Street's use of multilateral trade agreements to change the rules of global commerce in ways that favor the consolidation of global corporate rule. According to the celebratory globalization story told by Wall Street free-traders, *Multilateral trade agreements are bringing universal peace, democracy, and prosperity to all the world's peoples and nations by eliminating barriers to the free flow of trade and investment.*

They hoped no one would notice what free trade agreements are really about: *freeing the global corporations that control international trade and investment from legal restrictions on their ability to maximize the extraction of wealth wherever they see an opportunity.* An initially small group of citizen activists and labor unions from around the world broke the silence and spread the real story.

A powerful social movement was born that came to refer to itself as global civil society. It organized the Seattle protest that stalled the World Trade Organization negotiations in 1999, and it mobilized millions of people in subsequent protests wherever corporate elites met with national political leaders and bureaucrats to negotiate away the people's rights.[1]

When global civil society mobilized more than 10 million people on February 15, 2003, to protest the anticipated U.S. invasion of Iraq, a *New York Times* article dubbed it the second global superpower.[2] Made possible by the Internet, it was the largest, most inclusive, and most global expression of public opinion in human history. The demonstration failed to stop the invasion of Iraq by an administration that refused to be swayed by military intelligence, logic, or public opinion. That administration, however, has now been replaced by a new administration led by a black man with an odd name, exceptional ability, and a multicultural worldview who opposed the invasion. That, in my view, counts as a national and global victory for civil society.

The movement has created broad public awareness of the fallacies of Wall Street's globalization story. It is, however, but a subtheme of a larger Wall Street narrative: *Money is wealth, and Wall Street is a powerful engine of wealth creation that enriches us all.* We must now challenge the larger story as well and replace it with the real story: *Wall Street produces only phantom wealth that creates claims against the real wealth produced by others without itself producing anything of value. We have the means to liberate ourselves from Wall Street and to build, in balance with nature, a new economy dedicated to equitably serving the real-wealth needs of everyone.*

There of course is much more to the New Economy story, but this is the nugget of the argument to declare our independence from Wall Street, bring the promise of democracy to full fruition, and draw five thousand years of Empire to a close.

TWO HISTORIC INDEPENDENCE MOVEMENTS

The parallels between the independence movement that liberated thirteen colonies on the east coast of what is now the United States and the efforts of those seeking independence from Wall Street are both revealing and instructive:

As the colonial economies began to grow in their production of real wealth, their prosperity attracted the attention of the British Crown, which became more active in asserting its authority to increase its share of that wealth through new taxes and the grant of a tea monopoly to the East India Company, in which the king held a financial interest.

In the years following World War II, the equity policies of the Roosevelt New Deal created a prosperous middle class and flourishing Main Street businesses growing the real wealth of their local communities. Main Street's prosperity attracted the attention of Wall Street, which gradually asserted the power of its monopoly control of money in order to increase its share. It charged Main Street usurious interest rates and fees; asserted monopoly control of intellectual property rights, markets, and resources; and accelerated the creation of phantom wealth that enlarged its claims against the real wealth of the rest of society.

As the threat to their liberty and prosperity became evident, the colonists mobilized in resistance to the British Crown. Some colonists formed local resistance groups, with names such as Sons of Liberty, Regulators, Associators, and Liberty Boys, to engage in acts of noncooperation such as refusing to purchase and use the tax stamps that the Crown demanded be applied to all colonial commercial and legal papers, newspapers, pamphlets, and almanacs. The New England merchant class given to slave trading and piracy had no reservations about evading import taxes by adding smuggling to their business portfolios. When the Crown decided to assert its authority over the Massachusetts Supreme Court by paying its judges directly from the royal treasury, the people responded by refusing to serve as jurors under the judges.

Other colonists formed Committees of Correspondence, groups of citizens engaged in sharing ideas and information through regularized exchanges of letters carried by ship and horseback. These committees linked elements of diverse citizen movements in common cause across the colonial borders that had long kept them divided.

As the threat to their liberty and prosperity became clear, the people began mobilizing in resistance to Wall Street. They formed organizations with names like Direct Action Network, Public Citizen, United for a Fair Economy, the Ruckus Society, National Farm Workers Association, Art and Revolution, the International Forum on Globalization, and Rainforest Action Network. They organized Internet forums to engage in sharing ideas and information and to unite movements in common cause, reaching out even across the national borders that had long kept them divided. In alliance with similar groups in other nations, they mobilized millions in global demonstrations that regularly disrupted the international meetings in which the rich and powerful gathered to rewrite

THE PEOPLE LEAD SO THE LEADERS CAN FOLLOW

In the case of the colonists, most of what is described here was accomplished before the members of the colonial aristocracy we call the founding fathers met in Philadelphia to issue a Declaration of Independence and to assert their authority over a mounting rebellion that might otherwise have cast them aside as irrelevant. In the end, the rebels needed the founders to frame the rules and institutions of the first major experiment in democracy by persons of European descent since the Athenian experience more than two thousand years earlier.

Similarly, to achieve full independence from Wall Street, civil society needs its equivalent of the original founding fathers, establishment politicians willing to stand up to Wall Street, strip away Wall Street's hold on Main Street, and craft legislation creating a system of accountable, service-oriented financial institutions aligned with the New Economy agenda.

the rules of commerce in their favor and negotiate their division of the spoils.

The colonists also undertook initiatives aimed at getting control of economic life through local production. They boycotted British goods and subjected merchants who failed to honor the boycott to public humiliation. Artisans and laborers refused to participate in building military fortifications for the British. Women played a particularly crucial role by organizing Daughters of Liberty committees to produce substitutes for imported products.

Local Main Street businesses, workers, and consumers undertook initiatives aimed at getting control of economic life through local production and the patronage of local business. They organized farmers' markets, food co-ops, "local first" campaigns, local investment funds and credit unions, and consumer boycotts of big-box stores and the products of corporations that harm the environment and pay substandard wages. Local businesses formed national alliances like the Business Alliance for Local Living Economies and the American Independent Business Alliance. Local chambers of commerce disaffiliated from the corporate-dominated national chamber of commerce and joined these new alliances.

You get the picture.

Both of these historic resistance movements demonstrate the enormous and often unnoted human capacity to organize in causes larger than the self-interest of any given individual. They accomplished everything reported here without establishment leadership, support, or sanction. There were no organization charts and no central budgets. There were only thousands of leaders—millions, in the case of global civil society.

The organizing accomplishments of the colonists are all

the more remarkable given their inauspicious circumstances. They had neither motor vehicles nor any form of electronic communication. Their speediest means of communication was a rider on a fast horse.

The early colonial settlements had been operated as privately owned company estates ruled by their overseers. Many of the settlers were misfits and criminals forcibly shipped from England by a government eager to be rid of them, debtors escaping their debts, and rogues who came to seek their fortune by any means. Parishes were ruled as theocra-

THE POWER OF A LIBERATED SOCIAL SPACE

In many ways, the most important part of movement building is creating social spaces in which people regularly gather to share their stories and build the relationships of mutual trust and understanding that make effective teamwork possible even in times of extreme stress.

Much of my appreciation for the power of such spaces comes from my participation in the formation and early work of the International Forum on Globalization. The IFG grew out of a meeting of a few dozen of the world's most dedicated activists engaged in one way or another with what Wall Street interests were calling "globalization."

We came from many different countries with widely different experiences, talents, and takes on what globalization meant. Through the sharing of our respective experiences and insights, we were able to discern the big-picture story of what the "globalization" that Wall Street corporations had in mind was really about, and

cies by preachers who believed democracy to be contrary to the will of God. The colonial economies depended on slaves and bonded labor, and the family structure placed women in a condition of indentured servitude. The lands the colonies occupied were acquired by genocide, and their social structures embodied deep racial and class divisions.

Precious little in the experience of rebels who mobilized to win their independence even hinted at their potential for such radically democratic self-organization. Yet organize they did. Through dialogue and participation in acts of resistance,

we crafted a common language for communicating it beyond our circle.

Through our sharing, we developed genuine affection for one another and came to know, respect, and trust our differences, allowing us to work in common cause across great geographical distances with brief e-mails as our only form of communication.

Sometimes we acted as a group to hold teach-ins, issue joint statements, or coauthor papers and books. Smaller clusters shared resources to advance particular campaigns. Mostly we worked with and through our respective back-home constituencies, communicating our particular take on the big-picture story in meetings and through public presentations, publications, and media interviews.

Individual seeds of a new understanding were planted in many different places. They germinated, took root, and grew to create new seeds that multiplied with extraordinary speed. Within a few years, a powerful global social force was unleashed in an effective challenge to one of Wall Street's most destructive agendas.

they awakened to possibilities long denied, mobilized to walk away from their king, created a new political reality that changed the course of human history, and in the process learned democracy through its practice.

The historian Roger Wilkins named the decade preceding the Declaration of Independence the most important in U.S. history. In addition to drawing attention to the reality that we learn democracy only by practicing it, his words are a guide to those who would ask in our time, "What can I do?"

> The stunning achievements of the 1765–1775 period were not only instances of resistance to specific obnoxious acts of the British government but also key stages in the development of a continental revolutionary consciousness and impulse toward self-government, as well as the creation of the rudimentary instruments to carry out those purposes. . . .
>
> All of the practices and arts of politics were deployed in that fruitful decade. The colonists paid careful attention to public affairs. They spent time alone exploring and honing their opinions on important issues by reading history and philosophy as well as the latest correspondence, dispatches, and political tracts. They thought hard about what was occurring and consulted with others in order to inform and sharpen their views. They became involved in local and colonial politics by standing for office and putting forward proposals for action. When necessary—when, for example, colonial legislatures were disbanded, or when new instruments for protest and self-governance were required—they crafted appropriate new mechanisms. But most of all they thought, talked, debated, listened to one another, wrote, and created in ever-widening circles. All the while, their activities were fraught with great personal, political, and financial risk.[3]

The experiences that birthed the phenomenon of global civil society have had the same quality and serve the same ends, but on a far greater scale and with far greater diversity. They hint at our possibilities for creative, radically democratic self-organization now that modern communications technologies have obliterated the barriers of geography.

MILLIONS OF LEADERS

For the many millions of us working to create a better world, it is easy to feel discouraged by the seeming insignificance of even major successes relative to the scale of the problem. Consumed by the details and challenges of our daily engagements, we may easily lose sight of the big picture of the powerful social dynamic to which our work is contributing.

Step back from time to time; take a breath, look out beyond the immediate horizon to bring the big picture back into perspective,[4] and reflect in awe at the power of the larger social dynamic to which your work is contributing.

Making a Difference

So how do you know whether your work is contributing to the big-picture outcomes we seek? If you can answer yes to any one of the following four questions, then be assured that it is.

- Does it help discredit a false cultural story fabricated to legitimize relationships of domination and exploitation and replace it with a true story describing unrealized possibilities of growing the real wealth of healthy communities?

- Is it connecting others of the movement's millions of leaders who didn't previously know one another, helping them find common cause and build relationships of mutual trust that allow them to speak honestly from their heart and to know that they can call on one another for support when needed?

- Is it creating and expanding liberated social spaces in which people experience the freedom and support to experiment with living the creative, cooperative,

---

WHAT CAN YOU DO?

The first step in making a personal contribution to creating the New Economy is to take control of your life and declare your independence from Wall Street by joining the voluntary simplicity movement and cutting back on unnecessary consumption. Beyond that, shop at local independent stores where possible and purchase locally made goods when available. Make the same choices as to where you work and invest to the extent feasible. Do your banking with an independent local community bank or credit union. Pay with cash at local merchants to save them the credit card fee. Pay your credit card balance when due and avoid using your credit card as an open line of credit. Green America provides an excellent free guide called *Investing in Communities* (http://coopamerica.org/PDF/GuideInvestCommunities.pdf).

The second step is to join with others on initiatives that contribute to any one or all of the four activities mentioned under "Making a Difference" on page 181. Engage in conversations about changing our cultural stories. Facilitate new connections. Create liberated public spaces. Demonstrate new possibilities. Many specific possibilities are mentioned under the heading "Two Historic Independence Movements." Link your local

self-organizing relationships of the new story they seek
to bring into the larger culture?

- Is it providing a public demonstration of the possibilities of a real-wealth economy?

These are useful guidelines for setting both individual and
group priorities.

initiatives into national networks through groups like
the Business Alliance for Local Living Economies (http://
www.livingeconomies.org) and the American Independent Business Alliance (http://www.amiba.net).

Above all, engage in conversations about the realities of Wall Street, the difference between phantom
wealth and real wealth, and the nature and possibilities
of the New Economy. Be aware that economic reporting and commentary in the corporate media usually
reflect a Wall Street phantom-wealth perspective. Listen
with a skeptical ear and practice identifying the underlying fallacies. Invite your friends and colleagues to do the
same.

Join or form a Common Security Club for mutual
education and support in dealing with the economic crisis (http://extremeinequality.org/?p=92). Consider invit-
ing a group of friends or neighbors to discuss *Agenda
for a New Economy.* You can find a group discussion
guide at http://www.greatturning.org, along with links to
other New Economy discussion resources.

For all of the above, plus a wealth of stories and
resources helpful in tracking the larger movement to
which your work contributes, subscribe to *YES!* magazine and draw on the wealth of resources on its Web
site, http://www.yesmagazine.org.

The Power of Conversation

In closing, I want to share some thoughts on the power of one of the most common and seemingly inconsequential, yet revolutionary, of human activities—conversation. Every powerful movement for transformational social change begins with a conversation.

The women's movement offers an instructive example. A few courageous women started a process that in little more than a decade changed the cultural story that *the key to a woman's happiness is to find the right man, marry him, and*

POTENTIAL POLITICAL CONSENSUS

There is potential to build a broadly based political consensus around the New Economy vision. We can start with the fact that outrage against Wall Street greed and corruption is nearly universal. We also share a nearly universal positive concern for the well-being of our children, families, community, and the natural environment.

We long for a society that puts family and community values ahead of financial values, and businesses that put people ahead of profits. We favor global cooperation over global competition. We believe in equal opportunity and we want a voice in the decisions that shape our lives.

The values underlying our shared dream defy categorizations as conservative or liberal values. They are deeply shared human values.

It is our time to put artificial political divisions behind us and join with one another to make our shared dream a reality.

devote her life to his service. As Cecile Andrews, the author of *Circles of Simplicity*, relates, the contemporary transition to a new gender story began with discussion circles in which women across the country came together in small groups in their living rooms to share their personal stories.

Prior to these conversations, a woman whose experience failed to conform to the prevailing cultural story was likely to assume that the problem was a deficiency in herself. As the women shared their personal histories, each realized that the flaw was in the cultural story. This truth liberated those who participated in these early conversations to lend their voices to a growing chorus of women engaged in changing the cultural stories by which society had long defined women and their roles. Millions of women were soon spreading a new gender story that has unleashed the feminine as a powerful force for global transformation.

The voluntary simplicity movement organizes similar opportunities for people to share their stories about what makes them truly happy. The fallacy of the story that *material consumption is the path to happiness* is quickly exposed and replaced with the realization that *we truly come alive as we reduce material consumption and gain control of our time to devote more of our lives to the things that bring true happiness, such as nurturing the relationships of caring families and communities.*

Corporations command economic power. Governments command the coercive power of the police and military. The power of civil society is the power of authentic stories. Despite appearances, civil society holds the upper hand, because the power of authentic stories ultimately trumps the power of both state and corporation.

The communications technologies now in place create the possibility of melding our local conversations into a global conversation with the power to bring down Wall Street, lift up Main Street, and break the self-replicating spiral of competitive violence of five thousand years of Empire.

▶•◆•◆•◀

We humans have made enormous progress in our technological mastery, but we fall far short in our mastery of ourselves and the potential of our human consciousness. Failing to identify the true sources of our happiness and well-being, we worship at the altar of money to the neglect of the altar of life. Failing to distinguish between money and real wealth, we embrace illusion as reality, and enslavement to the institutions of Wall Street as liberty.

The implosion of the Wall Street phantom-wealth economy exposes how effective we can be in creating cultures and institutions that cultivate and celebrate the most pathological possibilities of our human nature. Let the ugliness that the implosion has revealed serve as an inspiration to finally get it right.

Our defining gift as humans is our power to choose, including our power to choose our collective future. It is a gift that comes with a corresponding moral responsibility to use that power in ways that work to the benefit of all people and the whole of life.

It is within our means to replace cultures and institutions that celebrate and reward the pathologies of our lower human nature with cultures and institutions that celebrate and reward the capacities of our higher nature. We can turn as a species from perfecting our capacity for exclusionary competition to perfecting our capacity for inclusionary cooperation. We can share the good news that the healthy potential of our human nature yearns for liberation from the cultural stories and institutional reward systems that have long denied and suppressed it.

The liberation of this potential is the larger vision and goal of the New Economy agenda. It begins with getting our values right and investing in the relationships of the caring communities that are the essential foundation of real wealth and security. As individuals and as a species, we can find our place of service to the larger community of life from which we separated in our species' adolescence and to which we must now return as responsible adults.

We can find hope in the fact that the institutional and cultural transformation required to avert economic, environmental, and social collapse is the same as the transformation required to unleash the positive creative potential of the human consciousness and create the world of which humans have dreamed for millennia. We are privileged to live at the most exciting moment of creative opportunity in the whole of the human experience. Now is the hour. We have the power to turn this world around for the sake of ourselves and our children. We are the ones we have been waiting for.

NOTES

Chapter 1: Looking Upstream

1. Bloomberg.com, "Follow the $7.4 Trillion: Breakdown of the U.S. Government's Rescue Efforts," http://www.bloomberg.com/apps/data?pid =avimage&iid=ioYrUuvkygWs (accessed December 6, 2008). The $7.4 trillion total was updated to $7.7 trillion on November 24 to include an additional loan guarantee of $306 billion for Citigroup. See also Mark Pittman and Bob Ivry, "U.S. Pledges Top $7.7 Trillion to Ease Frozen Credit (Update3)," Bloomberg.com, http://www.bloomberg .com/apps/news?pid=newsarchive&sid=a5PxZ0NcDI4o# (accessed December 8, 2008).
2. Jared Diamond, *Collapse: How Societies Choose to Fail or Succeed* (New York: Viking, 2005), 248–76.

Chapter 2: Modern Alchemists and the Sport of Moneymaking

1. John C. Edmunds, "Securities: The New World Wealth Machine," *Foreign Policy*, no. 104, Fall 1996, 118–19, http://www.foreignpolicy.com/ Ning/archive/archive/104/worldwealthmachine.PDF.
2. Kevin Phillips, *Bad Money: Reckless Finance, Failed Politics, and the Global Crisis of American Capitalism* (New York: Viking, 2008), 96–97.
3. For more detail, see George Soros, *The New Paradigm for Financial Markets: The Credit Crisis of 2008 and What It Means* (New York: Public Affairs, 2008), xiii–xxiv.
4. Ibid., xvi. I also recommend "The Giant Pool of Money," an episode of the NPR program *This American Life*, featuring interviews with people who had a variety of roles in the events that led up to the subprime mortgage meltdown, describing how it looked from the inside. Broadcast May 9, 2008; accessible at http://www.thisamericanlife.org/ Radio_Episode.aspx?episode=355.

Chapter 3: A Real-Market Alternative

1. The historian Fernand Braudel gives a detailed account of the origins and definitions of the terms *capital, capitalist,* and *capitalism* in *Civilization and Capitalism,* (Berkeley: University of California Press, 1982), 2:232–39.

Chapter 4: More Than Tinkering at the Margins

1. This comparative review of Sachs and Speth is adapted from David Korten, "After the Meltdown: Economic Redesign for the 21st

Century," *Tikkun,* November–December 2008, 33–40 et seq.

2. Peter Passell, "Dr. Jeffrey Sachs, Shock Therapist," *New York Times,* June 27, 1993, http://query.nytimes.com/gst/fullpage.html?res =9F0CE7D7143EF934A15755C0A965958260&sec=&spon =&pagewanted=7.

3. Jeffrey Sachs, *Common Wealth: Economics for a Crowded Planet* (New York: Penguin, 2008), 3–4.

4. Jeffrey Sachs, "Bursting at the Seams," a lecture presented at the Royal Society, London, April 11, 2007, and broadcast on BBC Radio 4, http://www.bbc.co.uk/radio4/reith2007/lecture1.shtml.

5. James Gustave Speth, *The Bridge at the Edge of the World: Capitalism, the Environment, and Crossing from Crisis to Sustainability* (New Haven, CT: Yale University Press, 2008), 57.

6. David G. Myers, "What Is the Good Life?" *YES! A Journal of Positive Futures,* Summer 2004, 15, quoted in Speth, ibid., 138.

7. Speth, *The Bridge,* 199–200.

Chapter 5: What Wall Street Really Wants

1. Bill Clinton, speech given at a fundraiser for Rep. Jim McDermott, Seattle, July 31, 2006, http://www.thomhartmann.com/index .php?option=com_content&task=view&id=408&Itemid=119.

2. Paul Krugman, *The Conscience of a Liberal* (New York: W. W. Norton, 2007), 5–6.

3. Phillips, *Bad Money,* 31–32 (see chap. 2, n. 2).

4. Ibid., 6.

5. Ibid., 45.

6. Ibid., 45–46.

7. Sarah Anderson et al., "Executive Excess 2008: How Average Taxpayers Subsidize Runaway Pay," 14th annual CEO Compensation Survey (Washington, DC: Institute for Policy Studies, 2008), 3.

8. Charles R. Morris, *The Trillion Dollar Meltdown: Easy Money, High Rollers, and the Great Credit Crash* (New York: Public Affairs, 2008), 139–40.

9. U.S. Department of Commerce, Bureau of Economic Analysis, "National Economic Accounts, National Income and Product Accounts Table, Table 2.1: Personal Income and Its Disposition," http://www.bea.gov/national/nipaweb/TableView.asp?SelectedTable =58&ViewSeries=NO&Java=no&Request3Place=N&3Place =N&FromView=YES&Freq=Year&FirstYear=1959&LastYear =2008&3Place=N&Update=Update&JavaBox=no#Mid.

10. For fascinating insider accounts of the way this played out and the underlying patterns of corruption, see John Perkins, *Confessions of an Economic Hit Man* (San Francisco: Berrett-Koehler, 2004); and

Steven Hiatt, *A Game as Old as Empire: The Secret World of Economic Hit Men and the Web of Global Corruption* (San Francisco: Berrett-Koehler, 2007).

11. James B. Davies et al., "The World Distribution of Household Wealth," December 5, 2006, University of Western Ontario, UNU-WIDER, and New York University, http://www.wider.unu.edu/publications/working-papers/discussion-papers/2008/en_GB/dp2008-03/. See also James B. Davies, ed., *Personal Wealth from a Global Perspective* (Oxford: Oxford University Press, 2008).

12. International Labour Organization, *World of Work Report 2008: Income Inequalities in the Age of Financial Globalization* (Geneva: ILO, 2008), 1.

Chapter 6: Buccaneers and Privateers

1. This historical review is adapted from a more detailed account in David Korten, *The Great Turning: From Empire to Earth Community* (San Francisco: Berrett-Koehler, 2006), 127–33.

2. *Encyclopaedia Britannica 2003*, deluxe ed. CD, s.v. "Morgan, Sir Henry."

3. Kevin Phillips, *Wealth and Democracy* (New York: Broadway Books, 2002), 11, 14.

4. *Encyclopaedia Britannica 2003*, s.v. "Privateer."

5. Ron Harris, *Industrializing English Law: Entrepreneurship and Business Organization, 1720–1844* (Cambridge: Cambridge University Press, 2000), 41–42, 46–47.

6. Ibid.

7. Edward McNall Burns, *Western Civilizations: Their History and Their Culture*, 5th ed. (New York: W. W. Norton, 1958), 467; and *Encyclopaedia Britannica 1998*, CD, s.v. "British East India Company."

Chapter 7: The High Cost of Phantom Wealth

1. Thornton Parker, *What If Boomers Can't Retire? How to Build Real Security, Not Phantom Wealth* (San Francisco: Berrett-Koehler, 2000).

2. John Cavanagh and Chuck Collins, "The New Inequality: The Rich and the Rest of Us," *The Nation*, June 30, 2008, 11.

3. U.S. Central Intelligence Agency, *The World Factbook*, s.v. "United States," https://www.cia.gov/library/publications/the-world-factbook/geos/us.html (accessed December 6, 2008).

4. Bank for International Settlements, "Table 19: Amounts Outstanding of Over-the-Counter (OTC) Derivatives," http://www.bis.org/statistics/otcder/dt1920a.pdf (accessed December 7, 2008).

5. Pittman and Ivry, "U.S. Pledges Top $7.7 Trillion" (see chap. 1 n. 1).

6. Shadow Government Statistics, "Inflation, Money Supply, GDP,

Unemployment and the Dollar – Alternate Data Series," *John Williams' Shadow Government Statistics: Analysis Behind and Beyond Government Economic Reporting*, http://www.shadowstats.com/alternate_data.

7. See, for example, Richard Wilkinson, *Unhealthy Societies: The Afflictions of Inequality* (London: Routledge, 1996); Stephen Bezruchka, "The (Bigger) Picture of Health," in John de Graaf, ed., *Take Back Your Time: Fighting Overwork and Time Poverty in America* (San Francisco: Berrett-Koehler, 2003); WHO Commission on Social Determinants of Health, *Closing the Gap in a Generation: Health Equity through Action on the Social Determinants of Health* (Geneva: WHO, 2008); Richard Layard, *Happiness: Lessons from a New Science* (New York: Penguin, 2005); and Michael Marmot, *The Status Syndrome: How Social Standing Affects Our Health and Longevity* (New York: Holt, 2005).

8. Bezruchka, "The (Bigger) Picture of Health," 86–87.

9. Ed Diener and Martin E. P. Seligman, "Beyond Money: Toward an Economy of Well-Being," *Psychological Science in the Public Interest* 5, no. 1 (July 2004), 10, http://www.psychologicalscience.org/pdf/pspi/pspi5_1.pdf.

10. Carol Estes, "Living Large in a Tiny House," *YES! A Journal of Positive Futures*, Winter 2009, 28–29.

11. Robert Frank, *Richistan: A Journey through the American Wealth Boom and the Lives of the New Rich* (New York: Crown, 2007).

Chapter 8: The End of Empire

1. This chapter is based on the historical accounts developed and documented in much richer detail in Korten, *The Great Turning* (see chap. 6, n. 1).

2. Riane Eisler, *The Chalice and The Blade: Our History, Our Future* (New York: HarperCollins, 1987), 66.

3. Ibid., 66–69. For a fascinating exploration of the forces underlying this early turn to Empire and the specifics of how it played out, I highly recommend Brian Griffith, *The Gardens of Their Dreams: Desertification and Culture in World History* (Halifax: Fernwood, 2001).

4. This estimate is from Internet World Stats, "Internet Usage Statistics: World Internet Users and Population Stats," http://www.internetworldstats.com/stats.htm (accessed December 8, 2008).

Chapter 9: What People Really Want

1. Portions of the following are adapted from David Korten, "We Are Hard-Wired to Care," *YES! A Journal of Positive Futures*, Fall 2008, 48–51, http://www.yesmagazine.org/article.asp?ID=2848.

2. For information about the Earth Charter Initiative, visit http://www
.earthcharter.org/.
3. Michael Lerner, "Closed Hearts, Closed Minds," *Tikkun*, vol. 18, no. 5,
September/October 2003, 10.
4. For the report and an opportunity to calculate your own Happy Planet
Index, go to http://www.happyplanetindex.org/.
5. Puanani Burgess is on the boards of *YES!* magazine and the People-
Centered Development Forum. She shared this story at "Navigating the Great Turning," a leadership gathering in Columbus, Ohio,
in March 2007 and in a subsequent personal communication to the
author.

Chapter 10: Essential Priorities

1. Originally published in Henry Jarrett, ed., *Environmental Quality
in a Growing Economy* (Baltimore: Johns Hopkins University Press,
1968), 3–14.
2. Glenn Greenwald, "The Bipartisan Consensus on U.S. Military Spending," *Salon*, January 2, 2008, http://www.salon.com/opinion/
greenwald/2008/01/02/military_spending/.

Chapter 11: Liberating Main Street

1. Adam Smith, *The Theory of Moral Sentiments*, 1759, in D. D. Rapha-
el and A. L. Macfie, eds., *The Glasgow Edition of the Works and Correspondence of Adam Smith* (Indianapolis: Liberty Fund, 1984), vol. 1,
218.
2. This agenda is adapted and expanded from David Korten, "Beyond
Bailouts: Let's Put Life Ahead of Money," *YES! A Journal of Positive
Futures*, Winter 2009, 12–15; and Korten, "After the Meltdown" (see
chap. 4, n. 1).
3. The Canadian International Institute for Sustainable Development maintains an online "Global Directory to Indicator Initiatives"
at http://www.iisd.org/measure/compendium/. See also Carolyn J.
Strange and Jason Venetoulis, *The Community Indicators Handbook:
Measuring Progress toward Healthy and Sustainable Communities*,
2nd ed. (San Francisco: Redefining Progress, 2006).
4. Sarah Anderson et al., *Responding to Main Street: A Sensible Plan for
Recovery* (Washington, DC: Institute for Policy Studies, October 1,
2008), 2, http://bailoutmainstreet.com/wp/wp-content/uploads/
ips_sensible_plan-v2.pdf.
5. Ralph Estes, *Tyranny of the Bottom Line: Why Corporations Make
Good People Do Bad Things* (San Francisco: Berrett-Koehler, 1996),
171–78.
6. Anderson et al., *Responding to Main Street*.

Chapter 12: Real-Wealth Financial Services

1. *Mammon* is defined by *The New Oxford Dictionary of English* as "wealth regarded as an evil influence or false object of worship and devotion" (Oxford: Oxford University Press, 2002, CD-ROM edition published by SelectSoft Publishing).

2. Ellen Hodgson Brown, *The Web of Debt: The Shocking Truth about Our Money System and How We Can Break Free* (Baton Rouge, LA: Third Millennium Press, 2008); and "A Radical Plan for Funding a New Deal," *YES! Online,* December 2008, http://www.yesmagazine .org/article.asp?id=3162.

3. The issues, options, and historical experience are examined at length in a number of important but little-known books, including Joseph Huber and James Robertson, *Creating New Money: A Monetary Reform for the Information Age* (London: New Economics Foundation, n.d.), http://www.neweconomics.org/gen/uploads/ CreatingNewMoney.pdf; Brown, *The Web of Debt*; and Stephen Zarlenga, *The Lost Science of Money: The Mythology of Money—the Story of Power* (Valatie, NY: American Monetary Institute, 2002), http:// www.monetary.org/.

4. Shadow Government Statistics, "Inflation, Money Supply, GDP" (see chap. 7, n. 6).

5. Gar Alperovitz, "Retirement Crisis, Real or Imagined? Moral and Economic Questions on Social Security," *YES! A Journal of Positive Futures,* Fall 2005, http://www.yesmagazine.org/article.asp?ID=1285.

Chapter 14: An Address I Hope President Obama Will One Day Deliver to the Nation

1. The following address is adapted from Korten, "After the Meltdown" (see chap. 4, n. 1).

Chapter 15: When the People Lead, the Leaders Will Follow

1. For more of this history, see Korten, *When Corporations Rule the World*, 2nd ed. (San Francisco: Berrett-Koehler, 2001), 307–314.

2. Patrick E. Tyler, "A New Power in the Streets," *New York Times,* February 17, 2003, http://query.nytimes.com/gst/fullpage.html?res =9902E0DC1E3AF934A25751C0A9659C8B63.

3. Roger Wilkins, *Jefferson's Pillow: The Founding Fathers and the Dilemma of Black Patriotism* (Boston: Beacon, 2001), 18–19.

4. Because this work falls below the radar of corporate media, keeping its scale and power in focus can be difficult. *YES!* magazine readers tell us that the publication is a useful tonic in moments of personal despair because each issue tells the story of the larger movement's growing power, scope, and influence.

ABOUT THE AUTHOR

D r. David C. Korten worked for more than thirty-five years in preeminent business, academic, and international development institutions before he turned away from the establishment to work exclusively with public interest citizen-action groups. He is the cofounder and board chair of the Positive Futures Network, publishers of *YES!* magazine, the founder and president of the People-Centered Development Forum, a board member of the Business Alliance for Local Living Economies, an associate of the International Forum on Globalization, and a member of the Club of Rome. He is co-chair of the New Economy Working Group formed in 2008 to formulate and advance a New Economy agenda.

Korten earned his MBA and PhD degrees at the Stanford University Graduate School of Business. Trained in organization theory, business strategy, and economics, he devoted his early career to setting up business schools in low-income countries—starting with Ethiopia—in the hope that creating a new class of professional business entrepreneurs would be the key to ending global poverty. He completed his military service during the Vietnam War as a captain in the U.S. Air Force, with duty at the Special Air Warfare School, Air Force headquarters command, the Office of the Secretary of Defense, and the Advanced Research Projects Agency.

Korten then served for five and a half years as a faculty member of the Harvard University Graduate School of Business, where he taught in Harvard's middle management, MBA, and doctoral programs and served as Harvard's adviser to the Central American Management Institute in Nicaragua. He subsequently joined the staff of the Harvard Institute for International Development, where he headed a Ford Foundation–

funded project to strengthen the organization and management of national family planning programs.

In the late 1970s, Korten left U.S. academia and moved to Southeast Asia, where he lived for nearly fifteen years, serving first as a Ford Foundation project specialist and later as Asia regional adviser on development management to the U.S. Agency for International Development. His work there won him international recognition for his contributions to the development of strategies for transforming public bureaucracies into responsive support systems dedicated to strengthening the community control and management of land, water, and forestry resources.

Increasingly concerned that the economic models embraced by official aid agencies were increasing poverty and environmental destruction and that these agencies were impervious to change from within, Korten broke with the official aid system. His last five years in Asia were devoted to working with leaders of Asian nongovernmental organizations on identifying the root causes of development failure in the region and building the capacity of civil society organizations to function as strategic catalysts of positive national- and global-level change.

Korten came to realize that the crisis of deepening poverty, inequality, environmental devastation, and social disintegration he observed in Asia was playing out in nearly every country in the world—including the United States and other "developed" countries. Furthermore, he concluded that the United States was actively promoting—both at home and abroad—the very policies that were deepening the crisis. If there were to be a positive human future, the United States must change. He returned to the United States in 1992 to share with his fellow Americans the lessons he had learned abroad.

Korten's publications are required reading in university courses around the world. He has written numerous books, including the international best seller *When Corporations Rule the World, The Great Turning: From Empire to Earth Community,* and *The Post-Corporate World: Life after Capitalism.* He contributes regularly to edited books and professional journals, and to a wide variety of periodical publications. He is also a popular international speaker and a regular guest on talk radio and television.

ABOUT BERRETT-KOEHLER PUBLISHERS

Berrett-Koehler is an independent publisher dedicated to an ambitious mission: Creating a World That Works for All.

We believe that to truly create a better world, action is needed at all levels – individual, organizational, and societal. At the individual level, our publications help people align their lives with their values and with their aspirations for a better world. At the organizational level, our publications promote progressive leadership and management practices, socially responsible approaches to business, and humane and effective organizations. At the societal level, our publications advance social and economic justice, shared prosperity, sustainability, and new solutions to national and global issues.

A major theme of our publications is "Opening Up New Space." They challenge conventional thinking, introduce new ideas, and foster positive change. Their common quest is changing the underlying beliefs, mindsets, and structures that keep generating the same cycles of problems, no matter who our leaders are or what improvement programs we adopt.

We strive to practice what we preach – to operate our publishing company in line with the ideas in our books. At the core of our approach is *stewardship*, which we define as a deep sense of responsibility to administer the company for the benefit of all of our "stakeholder" groups: authors, customers, employees, investors, service providers, and the communities and environment around us.

We are grateful to the thousands of readers, authors, and other friends of the company who consider themselves to be part of the "BK Community." We hope that you, too, will join us in our mission.

A BK Currents Book

This book is part of our BK Currents series. BK Currents books advance social and economic justice by exploring the critical intersections between business and society. Offering a unique combination of thoughtful analysis and progressive alternatives, BK Currents books promote positive change at the national and global levels.

To find out more, visit www.bkcurrents.com.

BE CONNECTED

Visit Our Website

Go to www.bkconnection.com to read exclusive previews and excerpts of new books, find detailed information on all Berrett-Koehler titles and authors, browse subject-area libraries of books, and get special discounts.

Subscribe to Our Free E-Newsletter

Be the first to hear about new publications, special discount offers, exclusive articles, news about bestsellers, and more! Get on the list for our free e-newsletter by going to www.bkconnection.com.

Get Quantity Discounts

Berrett-Koehler books are available at quantity discounts for orders of ten or more copies. Please call us toll-free at (800) 929-2929 or email us at bkp.orders@aidcvt.com.

Host a Reading Group

For tips on how to form and carry on a book reading group in your workplace or community, see our website at www.bkconnection.com.

Join the BK Community

Thousands of readers of our books have become part of the "BK Community" by participating in events featuring our authors, reviewing draft manuscripts of forthcoming books, spreading the word about their favorite books, and supporting our publishing program in other ways. If you would like to join the BK Community, please contact us at bkcommunity@bkpub.com.

OK, so now what?

 ## Go to

www.yesmagazine.org/neweconomy
for the latest *YES!* take on building a Main
Street economy that will work for all.

Subscribe

to *YES! Magazine* for in-depth discussion and
positive, practical solutions to the economic,
social and environmental challenges of our time.
YES! gives visibility to signs of an emerging
society in which life, not money, is what counts,
in which everyone matters, and in which vibrant
inclusive communities offer prosperity, security,
and meaningful ways of life.

*"YES! Magazine is the best source I know for
inspiration, information, and connections for
those of us who believe there is an alternative to
a world torn apart by greed and violence—that
for every 'No' there is also a 'Yes'."*

— David Korten
Board Chair, *YES! Magazine*

YES! is about solutions

YES! Magazine is a non-profit, ad-free,
quarterly publication printed on
100% post-consumer waste paper.

**To order, use the card at the back of this book,
or go to our website.**

www.yesmagazine.org